1. **DOWNLOAD** the Must Eat London app on your iPhone **FOR FREE** from the App Store. Scan the QR code to download the app immediately.

2. Go to **www.musteatlondon.com** and receive a unique activation code for the app. Following activation, your app will receive all the addresses from the book, including all the practical information and numerous extras. See which addresses are close by, add addresses to your favorites, find out how to get there...

MUST EAT

EAT

LONDON

MUST
EAT
LONDON

AN ECLECTIC SELECTION OF CULINARY LOCATIONS

LUC HOORNAERT
PHOTOGRAPHY: KRIS VLEGELS

LANNOO

When as a child my parents took me to London for the first time, I instantly felt the magic of this city. Most of my musical heroes came from here; the city exuded everything that I thought I recognized in the lyrics and riffs. This feeling is still present today. When PJ Harvey sings *On Battleship Hill,* I imagine, not the battle of Chunuk Bair in 1915, but survival in this urban jungle. And when I listen to Sting's rendition of the works of Late Medieval John Dowland, I think it is not about themes set in that ancient time, but about today's general beauty of this metropolis.

I have continued to visit London and its countless places to eat. In fact, I organised my very first *London Foodie Tour* a full 25 years ago. For a weekend, I showed people the best places to eat and where to buy exotic ingredients. Unfortunately this initiative was short-lived. Back then, people agreed over one thing: you can't eat well in London!

25 years later, everyone is finally convinced that, for some time now, London has caught up with Paris as culinary capital of Europe. This is where it happens; this is where trends are launched; this is where cooking at the highest level is performed; this is where restaurants will attract you over and over: you will eat Italian as in Italy, Chinese as in China, Japanese as in Japan, etc. This book is my homage to London: an enthusiastic thank you to this magical, dazzling city where I will always want to return.

Luc Hoornaert

LPQ NH FEB 26 10am ◯

CONTENTS

£: UNDER £ 15   •   ££: £ 15-30   •   £££: £ 30 - 50   •   ££££: OVER £ 50
Average price for a regular main dish and a drink.

CAMDEN LOCK FOOD STALLS

Unit 215-216, Chalk Farm Road - London NW1 8AB
www.camdenlockmarket.com
Mon.-Sun. 10:00-18:00

CAMDEN TOWN

Near to beautiful Regent's Park, Little Venice and the magnificent London Zoo, is the unique world of Camden Lock, or Hampstead Road Locks, as they are officially called.

Food stalls

The Locks are a twin lock system built between 1818 and 1820 by James Morgan and John Nash. It is the only remaining twin lock system on the scenic Regent's Canal.

Camden Lock Market is the collective name for various busy, pleasant markets where you can sample food from anywhere in the world. Next to the lock is a steel sculpture by Brit Edward Dutkiewicz.

In a way, the stroll from Camden Town metro station strongly reminds me of the atmosphere of Venice Beach in Los Angeles, of course without the beach and seashore. The ambiance here is alternative hip; there is always something to see: street musicians, boutiques and, what we are most interested in, countless food stands where everyone does his best to offer a taste of his homeland to the many guests. Camden Market has now become the third most popular destination in London. Initially, it was only open on Sundays, but with increasing success, most stands are now open all week although the busiest time is still on weekends.

Since the beginning of the market in 1974, Camden Market has truly grown into a phenomenon. At first sight, this complex maze is composed of six parts: Camden Lock Market, The Stables, Camden Lock Village, The Buck Street Market, Inverness Street Market, and The Electric Ballroom, a nightclub from the fifties converted into an indoor market.

If you look carefully around Camden Lock Market, you will notice many large warehouses. They date from the beginning of the seventies when the canal was still operating as a heavily sailed trade route. There were also plans to build a motorway across the canal. The result was that commerce reached rock bottom: who would want to invest in an area that was doomed to disappear? When in 1976 the motorway plans were permanently abandoned, the market, opened in 1974, rapidly prospered.

For me, browsing Camden Lock Market is the ideal manner to spend nice, sunny days sampling all sorts of delicacies and enjoying the unique atmosphere. Note that on Sunday afternoons, the Camden Town metro is only an exit.

HACHÉ

stopoissoncodavo at**haché** ...arellacourgetteh

Haché, e [adj] a (pronounced ashay) vt minced viande.
derives from the French "to chop".
At Haché we like to make life as simple as possible, by using only the finest and freshest
ingredients in everything we produce.
We are constantly creating original and delicious burgers based on a simple,
traditional technique.
"At Haché, we have become experts in preparing and cooking a range of
vegetable burgers and 100% prime Scotch beef steak burgers in our own
way that ensures your burger is perfect,...."

Bon Appetit!

HACHÉ

24 Inverness Street, Camden Town - Greater London NW1 7HJ
T +44 20 7485 9100 - www.hacheburgers.com
Mon.-Thu. 12:00-22:30, Fri.-Sat. 12:00-23:00, Sun. 12:00-22:00

 CAMDEN TOWN

Sue and Berry Casey: two like-minded people who are madly in love with each other. They often travel to the South of France, mostly to Provence, where they feel like God in France every time. However, every time, they also return to their beloved Camden Town, where they opened a French crêperie in 1999.

Haché Cheeseburger

And with success, it seems, judging from the line of waiting customers, that very often goes around the corner.

But the Burger drawing factor was calling: in 2004, they opened in almost marginal Inverness Street their first Haché with the intention to introduce gourmet hamburger to the general public. One of their first and most regular clients was Amy Winehouse; her absolute favourite was The Canadian.

One of my most emotional moments ever was the image of a poorly dressed father who took a three-day trip in a rickety bus. The man had saved money for one year to go buy a cheeseburger for each of his children at a McDonald's that had just opened in Harare. Ah, the magic of the hamburger.

Most people think that Ronald McDonald invented the hamburger, but this is not true. During their conquest campaigns, Genghis and his grandson Koublai Khan carried pieces of beef under their saddles. The friction tenderised the meat and the result was a type of ground meat. When Koublai Khan was in Moscow, eggs and onions were mixed with the meat, and the first hamburger was born.

Otto Kuase, caterer from Hamburg, is the official inventor (in 1891) of our hamburger, a round bun with cooked ground beef, onions, a sauce, and at the time a fried egg. German fishermen introduced this delicious meal to the United States. Or, was it Delmonico, a steakhouse in NY, where the menu included a hamburger in 1826? Or, does the honour go to Frank and Charles Menches who, at the Erie County Fair in 1885 in Hamburg, NY, emptied sausage and moulded the meat into round patties that they served between two slices of bread? The nameplate of Tulsa, Oklahoma, also announces: The Real Birthplace of the Hamburger! Here, Oscar Weber Bilby sold a cooked ground meat patty between two slices of bread at the 4th of July celebration in 1891.

In Seymour, Wisconsin, lived a large community of German immigrants; one of them, Charlie Nagreen, aka Hamburger Charlie, sold hamburger steaks at trade fairs and conventions: ground meat in a bun, that people could eat while walking around.

In 1940, a company that would change the food world forever, saw the light: Richard (Dick) and Maurice (Mac) McDonald opened their first restaurant in San Bernardino, California, on the corner of 14th and E Streets. Eighteen years later they had already sold 100 million hamburgers.

However, this doesn't keep Sue and Berry awake at night. Their hamburgers satisfy more than hunger: they are designed for the gourmet.

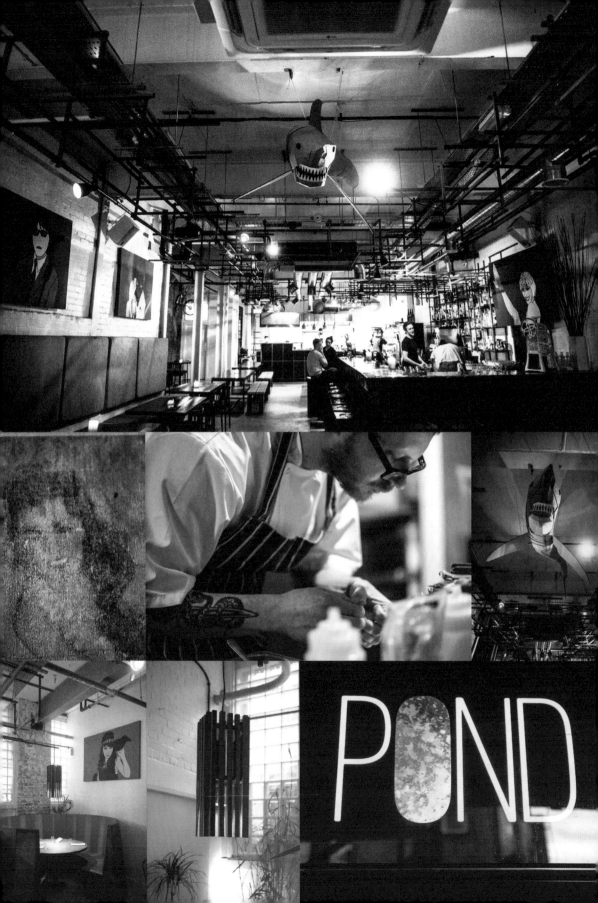

POND

Unit G2, Stamford Works, 3 Gillett Street - London N16 8JH
T +44 20 3772 6727 - http://pond-dalston.com

Mon.-Sat. from 17:00

≷ **DALSTON KINGSLAND**

Pond is the first restaurant in London that takes typical Hawaiian cuisine seriously
with the objective of charming and surprising the critical London public.

ALOHA

A raw salad.

Poke Ahi

Pond is located in an old Victorian building and has been very popular since its opening.

Traditional Hawaii cuisine actually does not exist because it is highly linked to the turbulent history and the immigration period of these islands. It is about pre-contact Hawaii, the period when Polynesian travellers brought their plants and animals to Hawaii and to the locals between 300 B.C. and 1778. The settlers fished and mostly lived on taro, coconut, sugar cane, sweet potatoes, and yam roots.

Following contacts with the outside world in 1778, European missionaries arrived and of course tried to impose their own food culture. From the whale fishers, they learned to salt and slaughter fish; the preparation of lomi lomi salmon is a typical remainder of this time. Plantations were larger and more important; consequently, demand for workforce increased. Between 1850 and 1930, Japanese, Chinese, Koreans, Portuguese and Filipinos emigrated to the

promised land. The introduction of their eating habits and typical dishes created a masterly mix, and as a result Hawaiian cuisine evolved in a wider direction. Hawaiian chefs worked hard on their signature cuisine until 1992 when they obtained a definition of local Hawaiian cuisine that could fully fuse with the various historical ethnic periods.

Ahi poke is a very nice example of this fusion. A poke is a raw salad; the verb poké literally means 'cut' or 'make small pieces'. Ahi poke includes the most important fish from Hawaiian waters: ahi, or yellow tail tuna. It is in fact a fresh mixed salad with marinated yellow tail tuna as main ingredient, completed with typical Japanese seasoning. The dish is complex, very fresh and amazingly delicious and flavourful.

This brainchild of Byron Knight is by all standards a surprising experience in a surprising place. The totally bare space is a great setting for a discovery of Hawaii's finest.

THE SEA SHELL OF LISSON GROVE

49-51 Lisson Grove - London NW1 6UH
T +44 20 7224 9000 - www.seashellrestaurant.co.uk
Mon.-Sat. 12:00-22:30

EDGEWARE ROAD

Even though fried fish was introduced in England by Jews fleeing from Portugal and Spain in the 16th century, fish and ships is now a highly traditional dish that will be forever associated with London and, by extension, with England.

Fish and chips

Fish and chips is one of the only meals that were not subject to rationing during WW II.

It became popular in the UK with the emergence of massive fishing in the North Sea and faster transportation, mostly by train, to the large British cities. We are talking of the second half of the 19th century. In 1860, Joseph Malin opened the first fish and chips shop in London: a shop with the genius combination of fried fish with the very first chips, located in Tommyfield Market, Oldham. So was the fish and chips born as fast food. In 1838, Charles Dickens himself, in Oliver Twist, talks of 'a fried fish warehouse'. It was also Dickens who first mentions fried pieces of potato, in *A Tale of Two Cities* dating from 1859. He wrote of 'Husky chips of potatoes fried with some reluctant drops of oil'.

The first fish restaurant would come a little later. It was in 1896, opened by Samuel Isaacs. In his car-pet-dressed restaurant, he sold fish and chips, bread, butter and tea for 9 pence and very quickly found himself at the head of a restaurant chain. By the 20th century, with the slogan 'this is the place', he owned thirty restaurants all over England.

Fish and chips is one of the only meals that were not subject to rationing during WW II. In fact, there is a story of Giuseppe Cervi, an Italian who sailed on a ship to the USA and accidentally disembarked in Irish Queenstown (now Cobh) because he thought he was in Queens, NY. From there, he went to Dublin. Giuseppe began to sell fish and chips to the pubs; from a handcart; his wife then asked uno di questa uno di quella (one of this, one of that). This is why in Dublin, in the popular language, fish and chips is still one and one.

The Sea Shell is a chippy with a more than 40-year old tradition. Only the black and white floor sur-vived a great fire in 2009, but like a phoenix, The Sea Shell rose from its ashes. The clientele is only made of locals who wonder how in the world I came here. This is still a place where older people dress up to go eat at their favourite chippy.

A beautiful, traditional place that should not be ignored.

NORTH

MESTIZO

103 Hampstead Road - London NW1 3EL
T +44 20 7387 4064 - http://london.mestizomx.com
Mon.-Sat. 12:00-23:00, Sun. brunch 12:00-16:00, dinner 17:00-22:30

EUSTON SQUARE

In our part of the world, Mexican cuisine is seldom taken seriously. What you are
being served under the name of Mexican food is often a true mockery.

Pollo con Mole Poblano

Mexican cuisine is probably the most underrated in the world. It was, however, the first to receive the prestigious UNESCO Cultural Heritage of Humanity protectorate.

Mexican cuisine is essentially a successful combination of native American cuisine with mostly Spanish influences because of the Spanish conquest of the Aztec kingdom. As true imperialists, the Spaniards tried to fully impose their cuisine, which did not really succeed, and eventually ingredients and cooking techniques spontaneously began to blend into a greater whole. With this, several local variants such as Oaxaca, Veracruz, and Yucatan emerged.

Mole Poblano is one of the world's nicest recipes: chicken thighs are simmered in a complex mixture of chicken bouillon, various types of chilli peppers, aromatic herbs, stale bread, nuts, and cocoa. This was made for the first time when nuns from the Santa-Rosa convent in Puebla de Los Angeles pan-icked because the archbishop was coming for a visit and they didn't have anything to serve him. In this thick, dark gravy, chicken looked mighty good.

Mestizo is the restaurant opened by a small group of Mexicans who wanted people in London to truly appreciate the value of their authentic Mexican cuisine. The term mestizo actually means fusion or mezcla, a term used to name the descendants of native Mexicans and Spaniards. This is undoubt-edly one of the restaurants in London where Mexican food is taken seriously. The tamales, very popular in Mexico for breakfast, are another example of this. This traditional breakfast meal is very simple but there lies precisely the difficulty. At Mestizo, they make delicious, sweet tamales called dulce de tamales. Corn dough is filled with, for instance, chocolate chunks, sugar, pieces of fresh fruit, or honey, then wrapped in a corn leaf and steamed into a corn roll. It has been prepared for so long that the history of its origin has been lost; in 1569, it was however described by the Spanish missionary Bernardino de Sahagún in his famous book *Historia general de las cosas de la Nueva España*.

Caramba!

TRULLO

300-302 Saint Paul's Road - London N1 2LH
T +44 20 7226 2733 - www.trullorestaurant.com
Mon.-Sat. 12:30-14:45, 18:00-22:15, Sun. 12:30-15:00

⇄ HIGHBURY & ISLINGTON

There are countless Italian restaurants all over the world. However, very few have been able to offer the genuine Italian cooking philosophy.

Black ink tagliatelle with braised cuttlefish, red onion and bay

The art of creating a fantastic, flavourful dish with few ingredients of impeccable quality is apparently not a gift to many chefs. During my many quests for brilliant Italian cuisine, I often wrongly trusted people who dared ask money for their Italian food; however, when you sit at Trullo, the only thing that will remind you that you are in London is the passing of a red double-deck bus. Therefore, I like to imagine the astonishment of Islington locals when, during their vacation in Southern Italy, searched for the perfect trattoria, which didn't seem quite as good as the Italian restaurant they know in their own environment at home.

Trullo not only looks like a classic trattoria: the food served here tastes as good as the very best in Italy, and that is in this area highly exceptional. Here, I only see happy faces at tables, and very focused people in the kitchen and serving tables. The team working here includes only the very best; chef Tim Siadatan first worked at Jamie Oliver's Fifteen, then at St. John and at Moro. The influences of these three restaurants are clearly noticeable in the meticulous, subtle preparations coming out of his kitchen.

The pasta, made daily right before the beginning of service, are clearly the crowd-puller. Indeed, they are prepared exactly as you imagine in your wildest dreams of Italian gastronomy. Bite, balance between sauce and pasta, texture: it is the perfect plate. A lot of work came into keeping the whole experience affordable, because that also is part of a trattoria experience.

Alas, I do not have the good fortune of having a Trullo restaurant in my neighbourhood.

Venez donc, ma bonne amie!

OSLO COURT

Charlbert Street - London NW8 7EN
T +44 20 7722 8795

Mon.-Sat. 12:30-14:30 and 19:00-23:00

ST. JOHN'S WOOD

Oslo Court is a unique restaurant. You could say it's the Antichrist of hip, modern, trendy restaurants.

- PINK -

Beef Wellington

Since it is difficult to prepare, you do not find it often on restaurant menus.

It was started during the Second World War and has undergone several reincarnations. However, it has not changed since 1977.

This restaurant is not for 'neophiles', people who prefer to be the very first to try a new restaurant so they can brag about it everywhere. The type of people who think that every restaurant must still smell like wet paint and that handymen finishing the job are part of the décor. Then, there are those who are upset because the restaurant is so new that you can't make a reservation through Facebook yet. Imagine: you are finally sitting, before everyone else, in a hot-spot-to-be and none of your social-media friends can 'like' that you are there. No: this is a restaurant for people who are strolling around beautiful Regent's park and suddenly realize that they have entered through a wormhole into a different culinary space-time continuum. Welcome to the world of Oslo Court and the Sanchez Brothers.

This is a world where ladies receive a menu without prices, and were napkins are a pretty rose colour. The supplier of cream and butter can afford a week

vacation in a luxury resort every year, judging from the sole quantity used here in Oslo Court. Here, grapefruit is still grilled with brown sugar, and the colour of the cocktail sauce is at least as pink as the colour of the napkins.

Finding the restaurant for the first time is not easy: it is located on the bottom floor of a residential block of flats. The advantage is that throughout the years, the clientele has been secured and every time a customer came to celebrate his birthday in the restaurant, at least 80 candles had to be blown.

Arthur Wellesley, the first Count of Wellington, was mad about a dish made of a nice piece of beef, mushrooms, Madeira sauce, a little foie gras, all wrapped in puff pastry and baked. The dish would receive his name and enter history as Beef Wellington. It has become a true classic and, when perfectly prepared, it is a dish of supernal level. Since it is difficult to prepare, you do not find it often on restaurant menus. Beef Wellington always gives me a very good feeling: a feeling of homely pleasure and true comfort food.

ADDITIONAL EATERIES
NORTH

19 NUMARA BOS CIRRIK - £
34 Stoke Newington Road
London N16 7XJ
T +44 20 7249 0400
www.cirrik1.co.uk
⊖ Dalston Kingsland RR
▸ Kebab

ARANCINI FACTORY CAFÉ - £
115A Kentish Town Road
London NW1 8PB
T +44 20 3583 2242
www.arrancinibrothers.com
⊖ Camden Town
▸ Arancini Balls Wrap

KILBURN IRONWORKS BAR & GRILL - ££
332 Kilburn High Road
London NW6 2QN
T +44 20 7624 7341
www.kilburnironworks.co.uk
⊖ Kilburn
▸ Rare breed Ribeye Steak with Chips and rocket Salad

E. PELLICCI

332 Bethnal Green Road - London E2 0AG
T +44 20 7739 4873

06:30-16:00

🚇 BETHNAL GREEN

This pocket-size Italian café furnished with Formica tables is a true monument in East London.
The Pellicci family has run this place with heart and soul since 1900. Here, we are still
very far from the 'Starbucks café' style.

Cannelloni della mama
with double cooked handcut chips

It could be compared to entering a time capsule, and everyone knows how pleasant that would be.

The building was classified as a protected monument a few years ago. It actually almost has the look of industrial archaeology, since the interior décor and the feel are a rare example of the type of Italian cafés that flourished in London after the First World War. The emergence of a new style and generation of cafés doesn't seem to have affected them.

The social cohesion and creativity enclaves found in this type of café cannot be replaced by the gigantic coffee outlet cloned from one another. No, this is a culture form in its own right, a unique universe without ersatz atmosphere. The interior is packed with tables that are all occupied, and every time one customer gets up, he is replaced by a new candidate. In the middle of this chaotic shouting to the kitchen in Italian and twirling trays with the meals ordered, all you can see is happy, laughing faces. And within this chaos, the owners see a sort of higher form of order, their own order.

Everyone knows Nevio, who is in his early 80s. He was born above the café in 1926 and has secured his succession with his son Nevio Junior and his daughter Anna. Over the years, he has developed a true fan club and still looks terrific. And so it happened that one of his regular clients rode by one night at 11 and found strange to see light in the kitchen. He called the police and thus saved the business from a devastating fire. This is true neighbour solidarity.

Real family businesses are a lot of work, but to really understand how a family business operates, you should first visit E. Pellicci; there, you will see and feel what it is all about. Nevio met his wife Maria when she was sent to London by the community of the Tuscany village where they both came from, to help Nevio.

They have never opened the café 1 minute later than six thirty in the morning, always with a little Capitol radio or Sinatra tune as musical décor. And even then, at that insanely early hour, there are clients standing with their nose against the window. Bob, a taxi driver, invariably comes by on Saturday morning at six thirty, after his shift, to eat a plate of spaghetti at Pellicci's. The Gallagher Brothers were here also and had nothing but praise for this fountain of authenticity. The ambiance that reigns here is usually found only in small osterias in even smaller Italian villages.

This type of business, and this type of people are unfortunately threatened with extinction. Nevio doesn't think of retiring yet. 'What else could I do all day long?' he asks philosophically. Or, as a regular told Nevio after a royal breakfast: 'I always thought, Nevio, either you are in an institution or you are part of a home...'

G. KELLY

526 Roman Road Market, Bow - London E3 5ES
T +44 20 7739 3603 - http://gkelly.london
Mon. 11:00-15:00, Thu.-Wed. 10:00-15:00, Thu. 10:00-15:30, Fri. 10:00-19:00, Sat. 10:00-17:30

BETHNAL GREEN

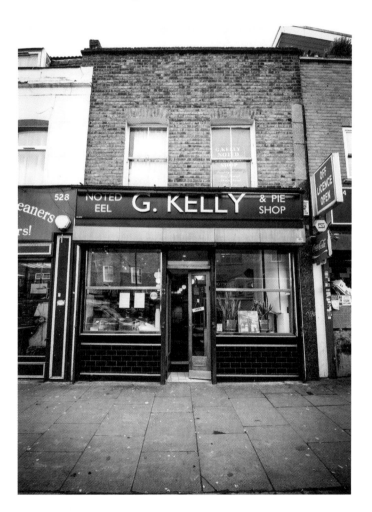

In the middle of the 19th century, the London scene was highly determined by the numerous street vendors who tried to offer their specialities to the passers-by.

Traditional beef pie, mash en liquor

A simple gravy made with fresh parsley, salt, and water

The most popular food stands were those which offered eel stew or jellied eels, closely followed by pea soup and of course the Street Pie Men. Eel was brought to London by Dutch fishermen who sailed the Thames to Billingsgate where the fish was processed, and offered to customers through more than 500 eel stands. The Pie Men primarily sold whatever wife or mother made, and it was customary to toss a coin to receive a pie. If the stand owner won the toss, he kept the coin; if the customer won, he received the pie and the coin.

To expand their market share, some smart merchants joined forces and offered eel as well as pie. Liquor was added to both dishes as sauce. This is why the combination made so much sense. Some merchants saw the opportunity and created an Eel & Pie shop. The poor people, who didn't always have food to cook at home, found their salvation in these rudimentary but pleasant Eel & Pie shops.

Samuel Robert Kelly was a tram guard who had become disabled as a result of an accident. With the small amount of money he collected by way of com-

pensation, he opened an Eel & Pie shop in Bethnal Green. He had 4 children: Samuel, Matilda, Joe, and George. The latter is the founder of G. Kelly, where we are today.

Although their route was not always a bed of roses, this typically British restaurant is still alive and kicking today.

The menu is very limited but every dish is prepared with great expertise and simplicity. Their eel dishes, truly excellent, still come from traditional Barney in Billingsgate. The pie & mash are of course house-made, and are a staple. The liquor is also house-made and, contrary to what the name suggests, does not contain alcohol. It is a simple gravy made with fresh parsley, salt, and water, lightly bound with flour. You can add vinegar and pepper to your taste.

Places like this G. Kelly counterbalance the ever trendier London, a proof that simple, traditional dishes are still a solid base for success. Even though this restaurant opened in 1937, there are still people who discover it every day. Find a seat here, and savour a piece of London history.

STORY DELI

123 Bethnal Green Road - London E2 7DG
T +44 79 1819 7352 - www.storydeli.com

Open every day

BETHNAL GREEN

The darkest day in the history of Italy is probably the day when a pizzaiolo placed canned pineapple slices on a pizza and put it in the oven. Nonetheless, the Hawaii pizza born out of a burst of creativity is the first choice of pizza in Italy today, probably thanks to the many tourists.

Pizza Margherita

Pizza originated in the Mediterranean where it was initially used as a plate. All other foodstuffs were placed on that plate and eaten. Only the most hungry ate their plate flavoured with numerous foods. Tradition has it that Aeneas, the Trojan hero, would found the city of Lavinium at the location where he had become so hungry that he ate his plate. The Vikings also ate a type of flat bread/pizza, a thin crust baked in an earlier version of a pizza oven, then covered with all sorts of edibles.

Pizza appeared in Naples in the 17th century, although without tomatoes or tomato sauce, since tomatoes where considered poisonous at the time. Tomatoes were introduced from South America around the year 1500; initially they were essentially yellow berries. This explains the word for tomato in Italian: pomo d'oro, or 'golden apple'.

In the 18th century, crossbreeding created the tomato as we know it today.

The best known pizza at the time was the Mastunicola, a pizza crust covered with lard, pecorino, black pepper, and basil.

For many people, the pizza Margherita is still considered the most authentic pizza. It was created by one of the most famous pizzaioli from Naples, Raffaele Esposito. He had the honour of making a pizza for King Umberto I and his wife Margaretha. Inspired by chauvinism, he created a pizza in the colours of the Italian flag (tomato sauce, buffalo mozzarella, and basil) and so the Margherita was born.

Story Deli is not about flashy interior and ostentatious proportions. It is about the essence: to prepare and serve the best pizza in London. In my opinion, they have succeeded wonderfully. Even though Lee doesn't dare call it a true pizza but rather a pide or flat bread with topping, I think it looks very much like a magnificent pizza.

I had my most memorable pizza moments at Da Michele in Napoli and at Seirinkan in Tokyo; both times, I felt that you do not need to be an interior designer to send your clients to pizza nirvana. The atmosphere here is coy and homey: a great place you will enjoy coming back to if you crave savoury pizzas.

The dough made of high-quality organic ingredients is rolled super thin and baked sequinned with insanely delicious topping creations. Every time, the flavour is amazing! The décor is surprisingly simple and unconventional. I find it very cool and cosy. The front door remains closed most of the time to let only the right people in. 'Knock on the door' is the message. Even though the interior does not entice you to stay very long, this is still a place where you will want to hang out a little longer.

It is no wonder East Enders do not advertise this small hidden treasure. This no-nonsense pizzeria doesn't even have a sign; this is clearly not necessary to attract people and make them happy.

ST. JOHN

26 St John Street - London EC1M 4AY
T +44 20 7251 0848 - www.stjohnrestaurant.com
lunch Mon.-Fri. 12:00-15:00, Sun. 13:00-15:00 | dinner Mon.-Sat. 18:00-23:00

 FARRINGDON

Fergus Henderson is one of the chefs who deserve my deepest admiration.
If I had known him when I was a teenager I would probably have had a poster
of him on the wall of my room.

Roast bone marrow and parsley salad

Nose to Tail Eating

For me, any visit to London is incomplete without at least one meal at St. John to enjoy a plate of home-smoked sprats at the bar. The pleasure is complete when, after a glorious meal in the extremely simple dining room, you gather the last crumbles of your Eccles cake and put them in your mouth.

When in October 1993 Trevor Gulliver and Fergus Henderson decided to open a restaurant, no one expected, and they the least, that they would change the world and become the face of a generation, of a ripple running through the world of gastronomy. This has to do with a few things. Trevor's eye fell on this building in St. John Street in Smithfield. In a previous life, it was a smoke house then a soy sprout farm as well as the Marxist headquarters. It was by no means a convenient space to host a restaurant; moreover, it was not easily visible from the street. There was no budget for interior decoration but the decision to keep the white blanched walls was conscious. No distraction! The food must be, and would be the primary focus in this restaurant.

From the beginning, Fergus' cuisine was wild, unconventional, daring, initially resulting in an impressive number of empty chairs. However, Fergus' furious talent and his tenacity to maintain the concept created a reversal. Nose to Tail Eating became a reality. A combination between the restoration of the traditional, impressive English cuisine and the use of every part, noble or not, of the animal into a flavourful, composed preparation. The rest is history. An entire generation of chefs has been deeply influenced by Fergus's philospohy.

His concept and his first cookbook became a gospel for numerous young and older chefs. Call it bistronomy or gastropub or whatever you want; I call it Fergusfood. One of his greatest merits is that nowhere else in the world did I see handsome, hip young people feast over a plate of chitterlings, pettitoes or his legendary Roast bone marrow. At St. John, one comes to take in the very flavourful Fergus style. St. John is not only an institution: it is one of the most influential restaurants in England whose disciples have spread over all of England and further, and preached his word in their own restaurants. During a vacation, I once had the privilege of working in the kitchen for two weeks. Only people who love to eat work there. Fergus wanted to teach us and most importantly share with us his deep love of real food.

A monument!

THE JERUSALEM TAVERN

55 Britton Street - London EC1M 5UQ
T +44 20 7490 4281 - www.stpetersbrewery.co.uk/london-pub/
Mon.-Fri. 11:00-23:00

 FARRINGDON

Who wouldn't love to eat a *vogelnestje*, a Flemish classic that is the equivalent of a Scotch egg as they call it in the UK? *Vogelnestje* literally means 'little bird's nest': it's an egg, big or small, nested in the middle of the dish.

Scotch Quail Eggs

→ A hard-boiled egg hidden inside a delicious, aromatic, and lightly spiced meatball

However, the history of this seemingly simple dish is somewhat deeper than one could initially imagine.

The world famous Fortnum & Mason claims its invention. It was introduced for the first time to an already critical London public in 1738.

The Single Hen Scotch Egg, at the time a small wink to the proverbial avarice of the Scots, was officially born. Detractors and realists swear they were inspired by nargisi kofta, a centuries old dish originating from the Mogul times, between 1526 and 1857. This narcissist meatball was made of a hard-boiled egg hidden inside a delicious, aromatic, and lightly spiced meatball simmered in a savoury sauce.

In 1809, this speciality became part of the British cultural heritage when Maria Eliza Ketelby Rundell published the recipe in the second edition of her renowned cookbook entitled *A New System of Domestic Cookery*. This book is one of the major staple books from the UK, referred to, then and now, as Mrs. Rundell's. Her version includes the inevitable gravy.

Today, the Scotch Egg has become the ultimate picnic comfort food as well as the ideal hearty snack accompanying a few substantial beers.

Solid beers is the motto of The Jerusalem Tavern. In a neighbourhood where many architects and furniture showrooms are established, this very nice pub looks as if it was teleported here from the 18th century using Doctor Who's blue telephone booth. This pub was originally located in the St John's Gate monument, now protected, then moved one hundred metres further on in 1720. It owes its name to its initial location as a tribute to the St John Knighthood who conquered Jerusalem in 1099 during the crusades. The original buildings date from 1720 but underwent a thorough facelift about twenty years ago by the new owner, the major St. Peter brewery from Suffolk. This recent brewery is already very famous in England thanks to its traditional brewing style. Their Jerusalem Tavern is a pub in every respect and clearly illustrates their love for the classic English pub style.

An excellent address for a sound pub experience. Sparkling beer and hearty, delicious pub food. If the small pub on the street side is full, take the alley on the left side of the pub and enter through the secret emergency entry to order your favourite beer.

SUSHISAMBA

HERON TOWER LONDON

SUSHISAMBA

Heron Tower, 110 Bishopsgate - London EC2N 4AY
T +44 20 3640 7330 - http://sushisamba.com/
Sun.-Mon. 11:30-23:30, Tue.-Sat. 11:30-00:30

 LIVERPOOL STREET

A Nikkei Burajirujin, or is it a Nipo-Brasileiro? In Liberdade, a neighbourhood in São Paulo, lives the largest Japanese community outside of Japan. The first Japanese immigrants arrived in this Brazilian city in 1908.

Samba Salad

Japanese/Brazilian gastronomic fusion

Following the abolition, in 1850, of slavery, mostly of black people, Brazil tried to attract other workforces to their country to work in their main export production: coffee plantations. They were hoping to attract mostly Europeans so as to make their country 'whiter'. However, because of bad work environment, several countries put a stop to immigration to Brazil.

In the end of the 19th century, the decline of the feudal system in Japan resulted in severe poverty and unemployment; consequently, numerous Japanese workers tried their luck in Brazil. This resulted in the signing of an agreement between Japan and Brazil for smoother immigration between the two countries. The first 790 men sailed from Kobe on the Kasato Maru in 1908. Almost all of them were coffee plantation owners. By 1940 their number had grown to 164,000; most of them arrived directly in São Paulo.

From 1920 to 1950, Japanese food in São Paulo was served in large refectories and reserved for Japanese people. The first real restaurant, in Liberdade, was named Okinasushi and opened in 1950; until then, the São Paulo locals were reasonably immune from Japanese influence. The restaurant changed this, and started a movement intended to erase gastronomic cultural differences in a smooth, harmonious, and friendly way.

Kiyomi Watanabe, whose parents were fishermen, opened in 1981 the first Japanese restaurant outside of Liberdade, precisely in Bladder where other cultures already had their own restaurants, including several Italian houses. Therefore, the Japanese/Brazilian gastronomic fusion is a fairly recent movement and had a slow beginning.

Sushisamba now wants to emphasize this fusion: he chose the 38th and 39th floors of The Heron Tower, the highest building in London prior to the erection of The Shard. It is rather a commercial office building, and the Sushisamba terraces are among the highest restaurant terraces in Europe.

Shimon Bokovza, Danielle Billera, and Matthew Johnson designed this beautiful concept in 1999 and completed it with a deep attention to detail. The basis of chef Jeff Kipp's cuisine are, of course, the Japanese classics, very nicely complemented by Brazilian and Peruvian elements.

A nice Japanese meal with upbeat Brazilian music and a view over one of the most astonishing cities in the world. It doesn't get any better!

TRAMSHED

32 Rivington Street, Shoreditch - London EC2A 3LX
T +44 20 7749 0478 - www.chickenandsteak.co.uk
Mon.-Tue. 11:30-23:00, Wed.-Sat. 11:30-24:00, Sun. 11:30-21:30

 LIVERPOOL STREET

Marc Hix is a talented chef who was the head of the Caprice for a long time. He was executive chef and managed sixteen restaurants in England as well as six others in more exotic locations such as Dubai and Barbados.

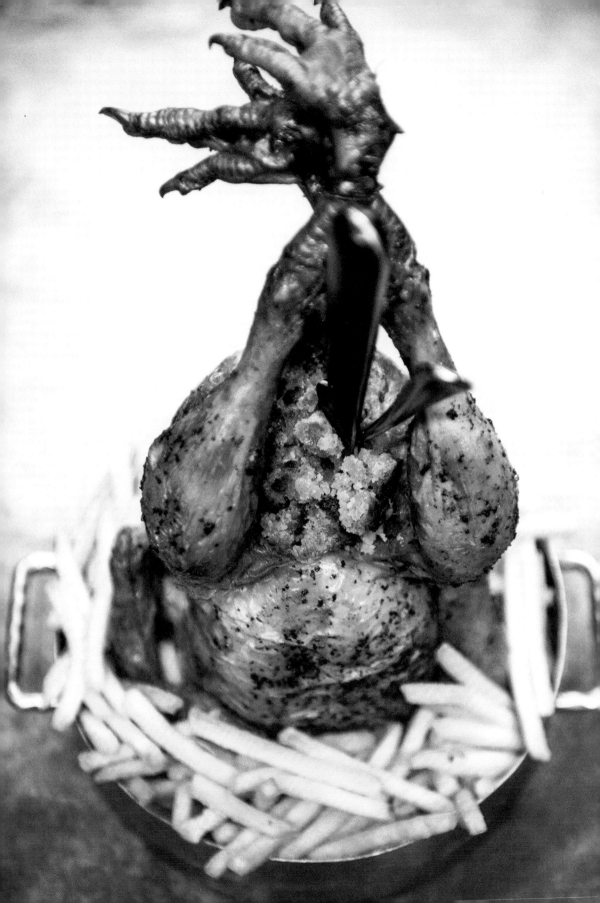

Roast barn-reared Indian Rock chicken with stuffing

The quality of these first class chickens is superbly showcased by the simple, pure preparations of experienced chef Rachel Hitchkock.

He opened his first own restaurant in April 2008. His most recent restaurant opened in April 2014. The Tramshed was an event: it was the eighth restaurant opened by Hix.

As the name indicates, The Tramshed is a restaurant located in a monumental old tram depot dating from 1905. Ceilings are high, very high, and this makes the space all the more impressive. The great crowd-pullers are two monumental art pieces made by Hix' friend and great artist Damien Hirst. Death is central in Hirst's masterful and controversial oeuvre. His best-known piece is undoubtedly *The physical impossibility of death in the mind of someone living* where a shark is pictured immersed in a bath of formaldehyde.

In the centre of this restaurant is a cow with a cock on its back, standing in a gigantic basin filled with formaldehyde. In addition to the cultural importance of a piece of this magnitude, it is also the theme of the restaurant: chicken and steak. Because, who doesn't like chicken and steak, Hix asked himself. This theme is also illustrated by another piece by Hirst: a cartoonesque work on canvas picturing, again, a cow and a chicken. Both works are very impressive.

It is hard to be any more obvious: when you enter the restaurant, you instantly understand that you will eat roast chicken or grilled steak. I always go for the chicken: for me, a high quality roasted chicken is always a favourite. It probably comes from my youth, when our Sunday menu always included a nice roasted chicken and that was always a feast.

In a kitchen without safety net, the initial quality of the product will make or break everything else. Here, the chicken comes exclusively from the reputable Swainson House in the Preston neighbourhood. These first class chickens are worth their weight in gold. Their quality is superbly showcased by the simple, pure preparations of experienced chef Rachel Hitchkock. They are placed whole in a nicely aromatic brine bath, then immediately roasted. The roasting juices season the filling made of breadcrumbs, sage, and onions.

The succulence and flavour sensations are unusual and more than a perfectly roasted chicken is not needed to guarantee a fabulous banquet.

EAST

BIRD

42-44 Kingsland Road - London E2 8DA
T +44 20 7613 5168 - http://birdrestaurants.com
9:00 to the late hours

 OLD STREET

Kris and I have been dreaming and pondering about writing a book on the most flavourful and unique chicken dishes in the world. Who doesn't love a nicely prepared, perfectly cooked piece of chicken?

Fried free range chicken

naughty but nice:
Only fantastic farm chickens, durably raised.

In any case, we share the love of a perfect piece of chicken with Paul and Cara, the driving force and owners of Bird.

Bird is a restaurant that should receive the 'worth the trip' icon in the red restaurant guide. You won't find better and simpler food.

Paul and Cara have spent a lot of time, travelled all over the world, and eaten fried chicken everywhere, all in the name of the science or, better, in the name of their quest to find the perfect fried chicken. They made a longer stop at Logan Square in Chicago. And on Sansom Street in Philadelphia, where they tried to uncover the secrets of the various fried chicken stalls. Of course,

their investigation also led them to several locations in Brooklyn, and they had numerous surprisingly great experiences in Asia. This extended experience was used to create a totally unique recipe elaborated down to the smallest details.

Free range and fried perfectly covers it and also describes Paul and Cara's philosophy: naughty but nice. Only fantastic farm chicken, durably raised, is used here. They are delivered fresh daily, which is extremely rare in the fried chicken industry.

Therefore, be prepared to try a best of version, a noble British version of the simple-looking fried chicken and I guarantee you will want to come back.

EAST

THE CLOVE CLUB

Shoreditch Town Hall, 380 Old Street - London EC1V 9LT
T +44 20 7729 6496 - http://thecloveclub.com
Mon. 18:00-21:30, Tue.-Sat. 12:00-14:00 and 18:00-21:30

⊖ OLD STREET

THE CLOVE CLUB

Magnificent Clove Club is located in beautiful Town Hall in Shoreditch, one of the trendiest, quickly emerging neighbourhoods of London. Built in 1865, this edifice has been one of the most monumental buildings in the area.

THE CLOVE CLUB £££££

Flame grilled cornish mackerel, rhubarb & toasted oats

Since the municipal services moved in, in 1960, it is also the home of a multidisciplinary centre for art and music, and with the arrival of The Clove Club, of gastronomy with a capital G.

The name and the building give it a posh, chic, and unaffordable feel; however, this is not the reality. Chef Isaac McHale and partners in crime Daniel Willis and Johnny Smith were once experts in a type of temporary food events or pop-up restaurants in parks, empty office buildings on Canary Wharf and in upper rooms of historical pubs.

McHale does not need luxury décor, English antiques or Japanese porcelain, or, most of all outrageously expensive, mysterious ingredients, to set your taste buds on red alert status. A chicken piece marinated in buttermilk and fried, caressed by a touch of pine smell, is more than enough to convince you that he is not the average trendy chef. This man is focused; this man is on a mission. His dining room is as soberly furbished as a cloister; it is almost Spartan: the only colour comes from the coloured tiles that separate his open kitchen from the dining room.

Although I hate restaurants where you can't choose from a menu, there are exceptions. Such exceptions are chefs like McHale: I absolutely do not care what they make, as long as they make something. Their signature dish, not a specific preparation, is the reason I am here. A chef like McHale is fortunately not to be caught in a pigeonhole. He is someone who doesn't copy; he also does not hide his inspiration sources. He is one of the rare chefs who can translate an inspiration into a complete form language of his own. Consequently, when I receive a dish of which I think that if it was on the menu I would never even think of ordering it, I must most of the times blame myself and carry out self-punishment because I could have missed it.

Impressive mastery and expert timing, combined with a deep feeling of cohesion between ingredients: this is all a chef needs to rise above the grey average. Many feel the call but McHale has been chosen. You should go there before everybody realises the wonders performed here.

LYLE'S

Tea Building, 56 Shoreditch High Street - London E1 6JJ
T +44 20 3011 5911 - www.lyleslondon.com
Mon.-Fri. 08:00-23:00, Sat. 18:00-23:00

⇄ SHOREDITCH HIGH STREET

In the emerging Shoreditch trendy paradise, a new jewel has been born. In the beautiful, iconic
Tea Building, once an avant-garde building belonging to the Lipton group, now lives a
breeding-ground for creative ideas and trendy settings.

Teal & celeriac

The building is located at the corner of Shoreditch High Street and Bethnal Green Road where you also have the entrance for Lyle's.

The chef here is James Lowe, who owes a large part of his career and influence to the pristine, white St. John restaurant; he was also chef in the Bread and Wine section of the trendsetter star chef Fergus Henderson.

When I took my first food trip to London, a full 25 years ago, everyone in Belgium thought that I had gone bonkers. To go spend a weekend of restaurant-hopping in London, the city that reeks of bacon and eggs in the morning? Those who were with me have never regretted it: just as so many young chefs today, I was already then convinced of the quality of the English culinary cultural heritage and of a treasury of high quality local products. St. John placed English cuisine on the map; others spread the word and carried on his work.

James Lowe has obviously not wasted his time at St John and has grown into a full-blood chef who doesn't need a lot of excess baggage to create a mature dish with his own, genuine form language. Here also, the menu is an ode to British gastronomic power and potential. Here, the motto is: treat every ingredient as most expensive caviar. Stephen Harris from The Sportsman showed Europe how you can let fish age: a technique frequently used in Japan but very seldom risked by chefs here. It inspired James to prepare sole to perfection. This is a chef with guts.

I also find his cod collar dish to have a true Japanese flair. Here, the meat from the fish rear jaw, which is very fatty and consequently of top quality is grilled at the bone and on the skin, and complemented with a little January King cabbage and some seaweed. Again, pure simplicity where taste sensation prevails.

Teal is a small duck that is fairly rare. It is amazing how much flavour depth is found in the smallest birds. This is the case with the rare preparations with teal, where James, once again, chooses to avoid the frills. Celeriac, perfectly prepared, seems to be the ideal sparring-partner here.

When James began to cook, his ambition was to open his own restaurant one day, and that is what he was able to do recently. At Lyle's, the goal is to process or mask the ingredients as little as possible. During his time in the St. John group, he developed a precious bond with several top suppliers with whom he works today. Through open communication and mostly by listening to them, James is able to obtain first class ingredients. In addition, his respect for hunters, farmers and other producers, he is highly regarded by them.

Lyle's is a very impressive restaurant without any unnecessary luxury. The feel-good factor is very strong here and the objective here is to offer guests a beautiful, somewhat intimate moment.

Wow!

EAST

THE OLD BANK OF ENGLAND

194 Fleet Street - London EC4A 2LT
T +44 20 7430 2255 - http://oldbankofengland.co.uk
Mon.-Fri. 11:00-23:00

 TEMPLE

There are still many people who, when they imagine an English pub, picture a sombre cave.
They have evidently never been in this pretty, clear, vast, and almost decadent pub.

Handcrafted pies

There were two pubs here, in the 16th and 17th centuries. In 1888, both The Cock and The Haunch of Venison had to leave room for the beautiful Law Courts branch of The Bank of England. This branch was only used by solicitors and judges; consequently, it was rather elitist, which explain the beauty and decadence of the décor. For 87 years, it operated as a bank branch before being turned back into a prestigious pub.

This building is not the only one oozing history. The undergrounds of the old London city centre are all linked together by an underground network of passageways and cellars. This is how the diabolic Fleet Street barber named Sweeney Todd (masterly interpreted by Johnny Depp) massacred innocent clients in his cellar, and then carefully gutted them. Through the underground passageways, he delivered the fresh meat to his girlfriend Mrs Lovett, who prepared it in delicious meat pies that she sold to unsuspecting clients in her small shop to the right of the pub.

Here, the speciality is still the tasty meat pie, also known as pie. The creation of the pie as we know it today is the result of evolution and improvements. The first people who made something that looked like a pie were probably the Greeks. The recipe was later adopted by the Romans, and spread throughout their huge empire. They also made fish, oyster, and more better-known young rabbit versions that you can still find in Italy today, in very traditional restaurants.

The crust or shell was usually thrown away because it was inedible; it was called box or sarcophagus, at the time a common word for box. In most cases, this 'coffin' was also the pot in which the dish was prepared.

One thing is sure: in the late Middle Ages, the French and Italians were able to improve the crust, thanks to the use of butter and perfectionist kneading and folding techniques, creating a pie version more similar to the one we know today. In 1440, the French Patisserie Guild in Paris made this dough official.

Etymologists argue over the origin of the word 'pie'. Both versions agree that the basis is the magpie. They assume that one of the main ingredients of a pie filling essentially consisted of the meat of the magpie, and that, consequently, the word pie originates from the magpie. There is another version: since the magpie steals things everywhere and hides them in his nest, the contents of a pie, also made of various ingredients, is named a pie by analogy with this magpie nest. Missionaries and explorers later ensured the worldwide popularity of this dish.

The Old Bank of England is most beautiful when the sunrays shimmer through the windows, casting a brilliant, almost magical light over the opulent interior. In this setting, the surprisingly flavourful versions of pies, accompanied by a pint of Fullers, taste even better.

ADDITIONAL EATERIES
EAST

BRAWN - ££££
49 Columbia Road
London E2 7RG
T +44 20 7729 5692
www.brawn.co
⊖ Shoreditch High Street (RR)
▸ Grilled Duck Hearts, romesco Sauce, calçot Onion

DADDY DONCKEY KICK ASS MEXICAN GRILL - £
50b Leather Lane
London EC1N 7TP
T +44 20 7404 4173
⊖ Farringdon
▸ Kick ass Burrito

GRAPES BAR - £
76 Narrow Street
London E14 8BP
T +44 20 7987 4396
www.thegrapes.co.uk
⊖ Westferry
▸ Sunday Roast

SONG QUE CAFÉ - ££
134 Kingsland Road
London E2 8DY
T +44 20 7613 3222
www.songque.co.uk
⊖ Houston (RR)
▸ Spicy Squid

YE OLDE MITRE - £
Ely Court, 1 Ely Place
London EC1N 6SJ
T +44 20 7405 4751
http://yeoldemitreholborn.co.uk
⊖ Farringdon
▸ Bacon and Liver

Behr's
Flash Cattle-Killer.

THE MIDDLE WHITE

Originating from Yorkshire, this excellent pork breed is highly regarded worldwide, with some Japanese cities erecting statues of these wonderful and unique looking pigs.

BROKEN BONES IN YOUNG STOCK

  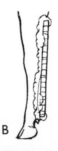 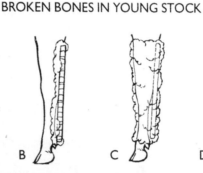

Two types of fracture.

A Prepare splint, a wooden lath is useful, cover it with cotton wool then apply bandage or sacking.

B Apply cotton wool pad to broken limb, then hold splints against the pad.

C Cover splint and part of limb with cotton wool.

D Bandage tightly to render limb rigid.

E Put splint at side of leg for break above hock.

SUNSTROKE OR HEAT EXHAUSTION

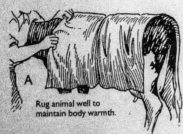

A Rug animal well to maintain body warmth.

C If sign of paralysis occurs, massage affected limb.

COW BRISKETS

Good Briskets.   Bad Briskets.

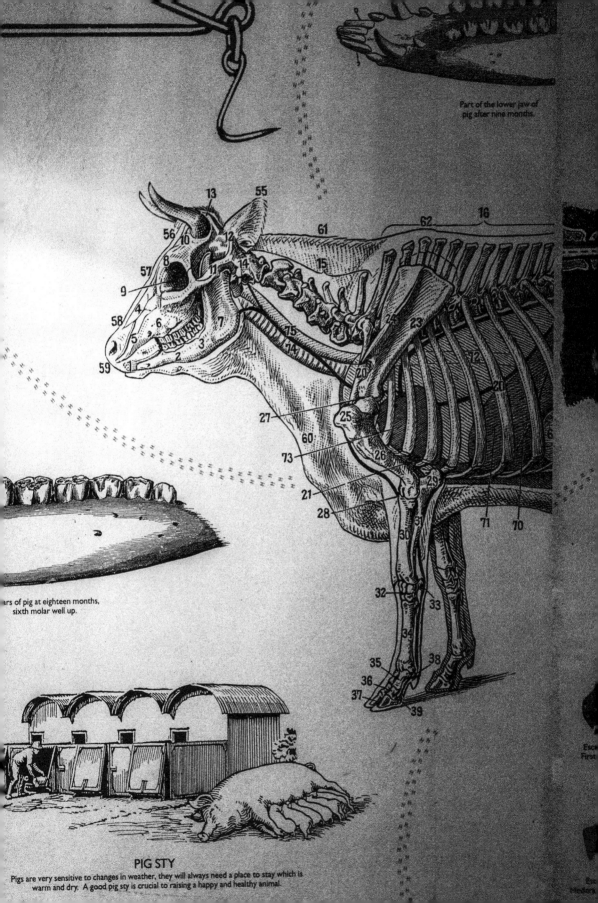

Part of the lower jaw of
pig after nine months.

...ars of pig at eighteen months,
sixth molar well up.

PIG STY
Pigs are very sensitive to changes in weather, they will always need a place to stay which is
warm and dry. A good pig sty is crucial to raising a happy and healthy animal.

AMAYA

Halkin Arcade, Motcomb Street - London SW1X 8JT
T +44 20 7823 1166 - www.amaya.biz
Mon.-Sat. 12:30-14:15, 18:30-23:30, Sun. 12:45-14:45, 18:30-22:30

KNIGHTSBRIDGE

The first time I ate here, I was totally blown away by the quality of their kebab, mostly by the almost liquid version that is removed from the kebab stick using a length of string; the Lamb kakori is really amazing.

Sophisticated lamb chops

The texture is rendered so fine by lengthy pounding in the mortar that it almost gives a liquid sensation in the mouth. It is unbelievably impressive even though we don't want to minimise the merits of other kebabs. The Kargosh ka seekh is a version made of wild rabbit.

Wow, phenomenal.

Anyone who thinks that Indian dishes are always scorching hot is totally wrong. As in everything, it is a question of balance, and that is what the chefs have totally mastered here.

Indian cuisine is one of the greatest in the world. The richness, variety, and depth of these dishes is unequalled. This modern, elegant Indian restaurant uses century-old cooking and simmering techniques so as to preserve the link with the entire, rich Indian gastronomic culture. In their open kitchen, they use mostly tandoor, sigri, and tava.

In Hindi and Urdu, the work tawaa simply means pan. It is used in the greatest part of South Asia, including India and Pakistan. The tava, or saj, is mostly used to bake a large variety of flat breads.

The sigri is a type of cooker usually used in Northern India. The cooker is most often firm and is essentially coal, dried cow pat, and wood. The sigri is often used by the very poor because they cannot afford liquid fuel.

In the winter, it also serves as a heating device for the home.

The tandoor is probably the most popular and best known Indian cooking method. Archaeologists found traces of the presence of tandoor in Northern Pakistan, dating from 9300 B.C. A tandoor is essentially a amphora-shaped clay or metal oven used to bake at temperatures around 500 degrees Celsius. This method cooks the meat in a short time, which keeps it very moist.

Amaya offers a new, innovative, approach to traditional Indian street food. To guarantee authenticity in his cuisine, executive chef Karunesh Khanna recruited all his chefs and kitchen personnel from the numerous food stands on the streets. Of course, he chose them where he particularly appreciated the food. Every new restaurant automatically brings something new: this is also true at Amaya. They call themselves a new type of Indian restaurant, and this is totally justified. The almost theatrical open kitchen offers a spectacular version of the tapas bar: a brilliant Indian kitchen with, here and there, a fusion element.

For me, Amaya was love at first sight, all the more since they master their classics amazingly well. Their sophisticated lamb chops, tandoori chicken chops and the tandoori black pepper chicken are so good that they should almost be banned because of the danger of addiction.

DINNER

Mandarin Oriental Hyde Park London, 66 Knightsbridge - London SW1X 7LA
T +44 20 7201 3833
Mon.-Sun. 12:00-14:30, 18:30-22:30

 KNIGHTSBRIDGE

Who is Heston Blumenthal? I cannot talk about Dinner without elaborating over the Heston Blumenthal phenomenon. Of course, there are the tedious technical aspects and the worldwide awards that this brilliant Jewish gentleman, with whom I share my birth year, has received.

Meat Fruit

When 16, he awoke one morning in Provence, he probably had no idea his life would take a drastic turn. Moreover, on that day he had an appointment with culinary history. When his parents took him to the starred L'Oustau de Beaumanière, he suddenly had a coming home feeling. He felt inspiration, not only from the quality of the food, but also from the whole sensual experience. The lapping of nearby fountains, the cricket sounds, the intense fragrance of blooming lavender, the atmosphere in the dining room while the serving personnel efficiently prepared food: he wanted to be part of it all. From that moment, he knew: he would be a chef.

When he finished school at 18, he decided to act upon the feeling he had experienced two years before, and he went to work as a trainee, without any education, with Raymond Blanc. However, one week was enough to abandon that project: he wanted the freedom to do other things. He took all sorts of jobs, every time leaving enough time for himself to learn the classic French repertoire. The turning point came

when he opened *The Science and Lore of the Kitchen* by Harold McGee. In McGee's stubborn philosophy, which questions everything that we find obvious, Blumenthal truly found himself; his life motto is: Question everything.

Another important aspect of Blumenthal's work is the fact that he found inspiration in the history of British gastronomy. He read *The Vivendier*, a translation of a 15th century cooking manuscript into modern English. It contained numerous unique recipes such as roast chicken that, when served, somehow seems to come back to life. The playfulness and creativity of the preparations in this book, combined with his scientific approach of questioning everything, were the first building blocks of this Dinner. His three mentors who, without ever knowing it, helped lay the foundation of Dinner, were Marc Meltonville, Richard Fitch, and Ivan Day. After extensive conversations with these three culinary historians, Heston began to develop dishes based on historical – often Middle Ages – recipes.

HESTON BLUMENTHAL

Ashley Palmer Watts has worked with Heston since 1999 and worked his way up to chef at The Fat Duck. Together, they have studied a great number of historic dishes from the Middle Ages and the Tudor and Victorian eras. He has been the chef at Dinner since opening day; despite its name, the restaurant is also open for lunch. The name also refers to the historic significance of dinner, which is the most important meal of the day that mostly took place in daylight, before the widespread use of candles and, later, oil lamps.

One of the most beautiful dishes underscored by this work and philosophy is the Meat Fruit. It is actually based on historic Middle Ages dishes, mostly from the period 1300 to 1500. It is in the shape of a plum, an apple, or a mandarin orange. The latter is a reference to the host, the Mandarin Oriental. The feeling that it is a gimmick quickly disappears after the first bite. It is a trompe-l'oeil, as is called in the visual arts. Even though you see a mandarin orange, very intricate,

the interior is an insanely delicious mousse of chicken liver with foie gras.

Pineapples are rotating with continuous slowness on a wood fire before becoming the perfect companion of the equally staggering Tipsy cake. This recipe was jotted down for the first time in 1810 and brought back to life in Heston's kitchen so that we can enjoy it today. The experience is difficult to describe because this dish makes you reach the limits of your taste buds and their comprehension ability.

In my opinion, Heston B is one of the rare chefs who will become immortal. He will be one of the chefs who will remain: the man who taught us to look at known things with totally new eyes, just like Paul Bocuse and Ferran Adria. The dishes are, of course, created from research, sometimes high tech, but they are mostly purified and appear simpler and more obvious than ever.

Hats off!

ZUMA

5 Raphael Street, Knightsbridge - London SW7 1DL
T +44 20 7584 1010 - www.zumarestaurant.com
Mon.-Fri. 12:00-15:00, Sat., Sun. and holidays 12:30-15:30 | Mon.-Fri. 18:00-23:00, Sun. and holidays 18:00-22:30

 **KNIGHTSBRIDGE**

The talented German chef Rainer Becker was born in 1962 in my favourite German wine region, the Mosel. His career took him through several top-class German restaurants.

Sashimi ———•

However, Rainer hankered after international experiences: he began to work in the Hyatt group as an executive chef, in Cologne and later in Sydney. His life changed course when he was hired as chef of the group's Tokyo location. There, he fell under the spell of Japanese culture, more specifically Japanese cuisine. This hotel was not only the set of *Lost in Translation:* it is also where Rainer found his true inspiration. In Germany, he had developed some experience with sushi; however, the simply perfect sashimi he found in the countless Japanese eating-houses blew him away every time.

He sunk his teeth into the details and focus of Japanese cuisine and moved to London. For a short time, he advised Alan Yau for the opening of his Hakkasan. In 2002, he opened the Zuma with Arjun Waney and Divia Lavani. The concept is based on his beloved izakaya: a meal composed of several small plates magically appearing from the kitchen in endless succession.

This magnificent Japanese restaurant is located in a small street, not far from Harrods. When you enter, you feel like being part of a large, exclusive party with only beautiful people in attendance. This is a sexy nightclub where the vibe is high in octane. However, it is also a modern izakaya seen through the eyes of a Tokyo design agency. Dishes arrive in high tempo: thrilling, fresh, Japanese, modern, and still deeply permeated by Japanese authenticity.

A show piece of the open kitchen is the Robata-grill, a very traditional item originating from the Northern Japan island Hokkaido. This grill is used, not only for cooking, but also for adding a typical fragrance and flavour to the ingredient; you could say the grill is used as a spicing element, with fabulous, subtle results. Of course, the sashimi is of more than perfect quality and freshness.

Sashimi is a very traditional element of Japanese cuisine. Literally, the word means something like pierced meat or body, and dates from the Muromachi period. Its origin could lie in the ikjime technique: the brain of a fish caught by hook-and-line is immediately pierced with a sharp pin so that it dies instantly, contrary to the slow death by suffocation customary to our world. This way, the meat is not as impacted by lactic acids and the fish stays fresh and suitable for sashimi longer. Usually sashimi is made of sea fish although salmon has been an exception used recently.

Take a seat at the sushi counter, at a normal table, or at one of the low kotatsu tables; it doesn't matter. Make your choice and fasten your seatbelt.

Of all the fish in the sea
I'm so glad you swam to me

SPECIAL
Grilled Pre
Served with

APPLEBEE'S

5 Stoney Street, London SE1 9A
T +44 20 7407 5777 - www.applebeesfish.com
Mon.-Thu. 12:00-23:00, Fri.-Sat. 11:30-23:00

LONDON BRIDGE

After shopping at Borough Market, I often come straight here. It is a very attractive place: on the front, it has a counter full of fresh fish where you can select the best catch and take it home. You can also have it prepared here by expert chefs.

Catch of the day, mixed grill

Inside, you will enter a small, cosy restaurant that only serves fish. If you want fresher fish, I'm afraid you may have to go snorkelling. I usually go for the catch of the day, perfectly grilled and served with a little olive oil and a salad.

This small, pleasant restaurant can be very busy, particularly on market days. Everyone, young and old, regulars and tourists, wants to find room in this small place to enjoy a meal. Fortunately, the few seats at the bar offer a little solace; in addition, you can enjoy the cooking spectacle from the open kitchen on top.

As it should, the fish is fresher than fresh and portions are really generous. How I love this type of no-nonsense restaurant.

SOUTH

BOROUGH MARKET

8 Southwark Street - London SE1 1TL
http://boroughmarket.org.uk/

 LONDON BRIDGE

Borough Market is undoubtedly one of the nicest and best food markets in Europe.
The quality and diversity offered here are of of an unbelievably high level.

Local vendors

Since the beginning of the 11th century, London Bridge was the gathering place for grain, fish, and livestock merchants; in the 13th century they moved to Borough High Street where they are still today. In 1755, the Parliament decided, for obscure reasons, to close Borough Market but the local inhabitants of Southwark would not let this happen. They managed to collect 6000 GBP between themselves and together bought the parcel located around St. Margaret church; it was named The Triangle. They reopened the market with their own staff in 1756. This parcel is still the heart of the market as it is today.

Over one hundred stalls at Borough Market have one thing in common: an unbelievable dedication to quality.

To be a foodie is evidently considered hereditary. When the daughter of a food lover friend turned eighteen and could choose a gift for her birthday, she resolutely chose to take an early morning train from Belgium to London with me, go shopping and take the train back in the afternoon, and prepare the purchased goods for dinner that evening. The customs officer had a strange look when my suitcase, changed for the occasion into a shopping cart, went through the scanner.

Here, I always feel like Alice in Foodie-Wonderland. For me, Borough Market is the ideal brunch stroll. The atmosphere is always very pleasant, and the food is stunning and so savoury. This is one of the best attractions in London.

ELLIOT'S CAFÉ

12 Stoney Street - London SE1 9AD
T +44 20 7403 7436 - www.elliotscafe.com
Mon.-Fri. 12:00-15:00 and 18:00-22:00, Sat. 12:00-16:00 and 18:00-22:00

LONDON BRIDGE

Any talented chef can't dream of a place more inspiring than Borough Market.

Smoked cod roe, winter tomatoes, baby artichokes

Here, composing a menu is simple. The ingredients will determine the dishes to prepare. They are so well prepared that the result is outstanding and very natural. Baking and roasting is only done in a wood-fired grill so that the focus is totally on the product itself.

The menu changes daily; even though it has a feel of improvisation or exercise, having Borough Market at your doorstep guarantees that nothing can go wrong in terms of products. Chef Adam Sellar has a strongly determined look in his eyes. In it, you read that if there was a cooking contest between two teams, and Adam cooked for the other team, it would be enough to look into his eyes to know that the other team would lose.

The combinations work wonderfully well and the simple, although beaut-ifully garnished plates complement the trendy décor where reigns an unbeliev-ably pleasant ambiance. The place is somewhat timeless and pretty, particularly when the morning sun penetrates the windows and caresses the bare bricks.

For me, Elliot's is one of these jewel addresses that you cherish the most, prefer to keep for yourself, so that you will always find a table whenever you feel like going. This restaurant does not have a signature dish but you will not miss it; Adam has developed his own form language, more than sufficient to keep the fascination and the amazement. Dishes have an intimate feel and seem to whisper at you and softly entrust to you their greatest secrets.

A hidden jewel of a restaurant, don't tell!

HUTONG

Level 33, The Shard, 31 Saint Thomas Street - London SE1 9RY
T +44 20 3011 1257 - www.hutong.co.uk
Mon.-Sun. 12:00-14:30 and 18:30-22:30

LONDON BRIDGE

The only thing that is a pity when you eat in The Shard is that you actually can't see the building. This architectural masterpiece and instant London landmark is proof that monumental architecture can really be beautiful.

Peking duck

|

Delicious duck dish.

Even in the toilet, with the best view in the world, I can only remember the Dirty Old River as The Kinks see it flow while they admire their Waterloo Sunset. From here, Ray Davies could have truly seen paradise.

The powerful, quality-focused David Yeo and his Aqua group from Hong Kong have natural experience with positioning brilliant restaurants in double-digit floors of apartment buildings. Hutong is on the 33rd floor of the monumental Shard and is the little sister of Hutong Hong Kong. The layout somewhat evokes the homeport with a lot of nicely designed dark wood that gives a typical warm feel. Both look actually rather identical, but the main difference is the level of liveliness of the dishes. Also, in Hong Kong, Hutong gambled on the exotic character by serving dishes from Sichuan and Northern China cuisine.

A hutong is a typical small street in Beijing. Because of the fierce and intense urbanisation boom in this city, hutongs have disappeared faster than the white rhino, and they have become a preferred goal of touristy adventure journeys.

The cuisine has a totally different character from most Chinese restaurants in London. Here, the cuisine is from the north of China where the most famous and celebrated dish is Peking duck. Roasting duck has been done since time immemorial; however, when during the Yuan dynasty a duck was prepared for the emperor, he was totally wild about it. The recipe for roasted duck is very old; it was written down for the first time in 1330, in a cookbook by Hu Sihui, a kitchen inspector for the imperial court. The first restaurant that specialised in this delicious duck dish, then called shaoyazi, was Bianyifang, located in the Xianyukou neighbourhood in Beijing, in 1416.

The recipe only became widespread during the Qianlong period of the Qing dynasty, when poets began to sing the praises of this amazing dish using all known superlatives. In 1864, duck began its conquer of the world after Yang Quanren, founder of the famed duck restaurant Quanjude, had improved the oven used to roast duck. Today, duck is really a symbol of China, and rightfully so.

Also, the Sichuan cuisine distinguishes itself from other Chinese cuisines by the use of papilla-numbing Sichuan pepper. Here also, the use of this pepper is slightly cut down so that it is acceptable for the gweilo, the stranger's taste buds.

Hutong is an adventure and certainly a formidable addition to the London restaurant scene.

OBLIX

Level 32, The Shard, 31 Saint Thomas Street - London SE1 9RY
T +44 20 7268 6700 - www.oblixrestaurant.com
Tue.-Sun. 12:00-15:00, 18:00-23:00

LONDON BRIDGE

Over the years, I have literally seen this fantastic,
magnificent building rise above the city.

Truffled flatbread

The irregular glass pyramid designed by Renzo Piano, who also gave us the Centre Pompidou, is a delight for the eyes. There are 72 usable storeys which makes it the highest building in the European Union.

In June 2012, this gigantic glass shard was finally opened to the public, along with the few restaurants included in this monumental structure. On the 32nd storey is the most ambitious project of Rainer Becker and Arjun Waney who already enjoy worldwide success with Zuma and Roka.

As a result, everyone expected an Asian-inspired restaurant; it was a modern version of a New York Grill. An impressive display of experience, since in 1992, during his stay in Tokyo, he had already launched a NY style grill. This idea came to them because the more they looked at the building, the more it reminded them of the Manhattan skyline. Initially, this ambitious duo had doubts; they didn't feel like opening a second Zuma in London was a good idea. In addition, they were not convinced of the impact of the Shard, not only on the London skyline but also on the entire city. The power of simplicity that lies in this project finally persuaded them to step on board.

The architecture of the building also inspired their choice of name for the restaurant. Oblix does not refer to Obelix and Asterix even if the large pieces of meat could make you think it does; it refers to the tapered, pointy shape of the structure, with a slanting, oblique line.

Fabien Beaufour earned his stripes at The French Laundry and mostly with the iconic Daniel Humm at Eleven Madison. He runs this kitchen with the precision inherited from his previous chefs. The cuisine, based on the concept of comfort food, is served to the guests from two open kitchens. Becker has eaten Japanese 6 to 7 times a week in the last fifteen years and, even though he is still fascinated by this cuisine, he felt it was time for something new. He wanted to bring here dishes as he likes them, exactly like Zuma serves Japanese food as he likes it. An other fun wink at NYC is the deli-style salad bar complementing the lunch menu. With of course, spectacular 360 degree views, the restaurant is very impressive, particularly in the evening when it's dark outside. Fortunately, the cuisine is just as stunning, especially the dishes from the grill, rotisserie or oven: a very high level and attention to the balance and the depth of the flavours. The menu captions are no literary tours de force which makes the tasting even more surprising.

An innovative restaurant with fantastic, attentive service and fabulous wine list: a beautiful, total experience.

ROAST

The Floral Hall, Stoney Street - London SE1 1TL
T +44 845 034 7300 - www.roast-restaurant.com
Mon.-Fri. 7:00-11:00, Sat. 8:30-11:30 | Mon.-Sat. 12:00-15:45 and 18:00-22:45 | Sun. lunch (set menu only) 11:30-18:30

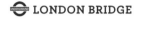 LONDON BRIDGE

Roast is here since 2005 although it seems as if this restaurant has always been a part of Borough Market. The building was used for storage and was totally unnoticed in the pleasant bustle that rules in Borough Market.

Slow roasted free range pork belly, Bramley apple sauce and mashed potatoes

Actually, they even operated a food stand on the market with a colossal pork belly & apple sauce. It is when eating this sandwich years ago that I came to know them. The building, named The Floral Hall, was dismantled in the 1990's and rehabilitated by the founder and driving force of Roast, Iqbal Wahhab. Roast has become one of the coolest urban restaurants I have ever seen. A sea of natural light flows inside through gigantic windows. Three 'walls' are indeed made of glass only; the fourth wall is an impressive open kitchen. The view is breathtaking. You look out on the fascinating movements of market-goers who throw themselves in the bustle of this ever pleasant and glorious Dickensian foodie paradise.

The kitchen is the lifework of chef Marcus Verberne and is a logical continuation of the inspiration created by the pioneer work of Fergus Henderson. Here, the no-nonsense approach is practically mandatory. Here, enormous energy is dedicated to finding traditional British producers, growers, farmers, and fishermen. The menu is an ode to these men and women who, day after day, defy the weather gods to offer the best possible products from land and sea. Only British ingredients are prepared in a fully traditional, simple, but always flavourful manner.

If there are still people who doubt the culinary richness of a city such as London or even the gastronomic qualities of the traditional British cuisine, I recommend they hurry here and put their feet under a table. The menu is a salute to good, durable, and genuine food, and that is what we all crave - right?

RASOI VINEET BHATIA

10 Lincoln Street - London SW3 2TS
T +44 20 7225 1881 - http://vineetbhatia.com - www.rasoi-uk.com
Mon.-Sat. 18:00-23:00, Sun. 12:00-14:30 and 18:00-21:45

🚇 SLOANE SQUARE

When young Vineet Bhatia was still a child, he didn't need an alarm clock. Every day, exactly at six-thirty, a very loud DC-10 took off from the airport next to their house in Bombay. Airplanes were his first passion, followed by his mother's passion: cooking!

Grilled chilli scallops, curry leaf prawn, cauliflower puree, Cauliflower fritters, peas thoran

His first dream, to become a pilot, never materialised because at 17, he did not succeed in the very hard physical tests necessary for practising this profession. He decided to devote himself to his other passion: to become a chef. Following his cooking studies, he went on to study economy at the request of his parents. His talent did not escape the talent scouts of the Oberoi Hotel Group, and they hired him in 1988. Growing up in culinary Bombay, a melting pot of various aspects of Indian cuisines, was a blessing for him, and inspired him to create his own form of language within the complex Indian culinary specificities.

In 1993, he moved to London where he though he would land directly in the Culi-Indian Walhalla. Nothing was further than the truth. Indian cuisine was the bottom of the ladder, and he decided to make it his personal mission to change that. The Star of India in Old Brompton Road first gave him this chance and he changed the menu so that it quickly began to attract a gourmet public. The reviewers were in heartfelt agreement: this man could make Indian food evolve and join in the game with the other important actors such as Japan and China. After an adventure with Iqbal Wallah, he opened Zaika, the first Indian restaurant to receive a Michelin star. In 2001, he stepped out of everyone's shadow and opened his first very own restaurant, Rasoi. Rasoi means kitchen: this is where everything happens in a restaurant. To be able to purchase the nice house in Chelsea, he had to incur large debts and even mortgage his own house. He gambled... and

won everything. The restaurant has a unique, intimate character; it offers quiet and integrity, exactly as one would expect from a high-minded culture like the Indian culture.

Vineet has since gathered a following with his interpretation of Indian cuisine. The man who came to London with nothing but his ambition and love for Indian food, has totally proved himself. His style evolves continuously, exactly as he returned the right to evolve to Indian cuisine in general.

In this sense, Vineet is one of the most important Indian chefs ever. His class and his ability to combine traditional flavours with texture and lightness, along with his surgical precision in the seasoning are simply brilliant. For me, a meal at Vineet's is always a fabulous moment: a benchmark for balance and for ancient gastronomic culture.

All dishes served here are his signature dishes. This is what happens with chefs who are greater than their restaurant. Their dishes are the signature dishes of an entire nation and of an entire generation. With the Rasoi Gourmand, Vineet gives himself nine chances to blow your mind. Trust me: no need to wait for the chocolate samosa to get there. No, this first-class Indian chef, who once prepared meals for first-class British Airways passengers, is a statement in his own right!

The best Indian meal ever: this is what you hear many people say. Who am I to contradict this? This is what I think every time I leave this place.

AMBALA

107 The Broadway - Southall UB1 1LN, Middlesex
T +44 20 8843 9049 - www.ambalafoods.com

Mon.-Sun. 08:00-20:00

⇌ SOUTHALL

Those who know me know that I don't really have a sweet tooth. I would prefer an extra appetizer or a plate of cheese to a dessert. However, there are a few exceptions...

Gulab Jamun

Thousand and One Nights feel.

I am totally crazy about gulab jamun. Alas, there are very few places where you can find it. When speaking about Indian sweets, people think of sickly sweet bites, drenched in honey, dull. However, the real thing will immediately give you this Thousand and One Nights feel. Few desserts are more sensual than a perfect gulab.

When my friend first told me about gulab, an incredibly juicy and sweet ball that, when you bite in it, drips a small trickle of rose syrup along your lips and on your chin, my interest was immediately aroused. Gulab is a very popular dessert/sweet in all of Northern India and is traditionally very complex and time-consuming to make. However, the result is one of the sexiest desserts ever.

I used to think, how difficult can it be to make gulab 'from scratch'? How could I know that every woman in Northern India makes this delight from instant packages or buys it ready made? My surprise was as great as when I learned that most Japanese women also use instant dashi. So I got to work. Very slowly warm up 10 litres raw milk during a full 4 to 5 hours until you obtain a batter with lumps, that can be perfectly scooped with a spoon. I added a little flour and with wet hands rolled the mixture into small balls. During the long warming process, I plucked 30 red roses one petal at a time, and cooked them in water and sugar. It was time to heat the ghee and fry the small balls to an even brown, dip them entirely in the rose syrup, then sprinkle them with some cardamom and saffron. Crazy work, but the result was insssaaaaaanely delicious.

Moreover, this delicacy has a rich history: we see gulab jamun for the first time in medieval India. The Persian conquerors brought a sort of small fried ball with them to India. The word gulab actually comes from the Persian words gol and ab that respectively mean flour/rose and water, referring to the intense use of rose water during preparation. Jamun is the Urdu word for the Syzygium jambolanum, a fruit from Northern India that more or less looks like this dessert. Today, it is primarily used in the treatment of diabetes. Luqmat Al Qadi is a fairly similar dessert from the Arab world, but with a totally different batter composition. The culinary historian Michael Krondl swears by all that is holy that gulab jamun as well as Luqmat Al Qadi are originating from Persian inspiration.

Ambala is a concept in the world of the mithai. It was founded in 1965 as a sort of branch for the famous Ambala Dairy a the border with Punjab. They brought their knowledge, skills and know-how to the UK where they now have dozens of stores. The quality has not been affected by their expansion, thanks to their dedication. Here, you see the top class mithai: kala jamun, halwa, besan ladoo, bedana, barfi, balushahi, rasgulla, jalebi, kheer mohan, rasmallai etc. Their assortment is enchanting and addictive. You can also easily order online and this is better to keep you under control, since when you are in the store you are lost and gluttony will inevitably take over.

CHANDNI CHOWK

106 The Broadway - Southall UB1 1QF, Middlesex
T +44 20 8867 7200 - www.chandnichowkrestaurant.com

 SOUTHALL

The Moonlight square, or Moonlight market is one of the oldest and busiest markets
in the old Delhi.

Aloo tikki chana

A happy and balanced marriage
between potato and chickpea.

Jahan Ara, daughter of one of the most iconic Mogul rulers, Shah Jahan, developed this beautiful square in 1650 next to their majestic red fort, Lal Qila. In the centre of the square was the chowk, a large pool that reflected the moonlight, which gave the restaurant its name. Today, with Delhi's urbanisation, the square is on the northern centre of this million inhabitant city and is still one of the largest wholesale markets in India.

Chandni Chowk, the Delhi neighbourhood, is known for his numerous traditional restaurants. Sukhdev's restaurant is no different. They serve very traditional dishes prepared according to time-honoured traditions.

For instance, the meat is bought only from butchers who use the jhatka slaughtering procedure. To produce jhatka meat, you must kill the animal with one single gash or stroke, with a sword or axe, for example, so as to sever the animal's head. This quick method is contrary to the slow slaughtering used by Jews or Muslims. As a matter of fact, our slaughtering method is very similar to theirs.

Here, I am under the spell of Aloo tikki chana, a happy and balanced marriage between potato and chickpea. Their house-made paneer has a nice texture and doesn't smell, as it should. The combination with chilli is truly amazing. Here, I prefer Indian vegetarian dishes that you actually don't see very often. The chaat preparation, popular in Delhi, has full play here in the Papdi chaat, based on large beans.

Their house-made halwa section also remains worth trying.

RITA'S CHILLI CHAAT CORNER

112 The Broadway, Southall UB1 1QF, Middlesex
T +44 20 8571 2100

Mon.-Sun. 10:00-22:00

≥ SOUTHALL

With shaking knees, I ring the bell at the lion's den. I'm going there to meet my future mother-in-law. I'm already regretting my idea of making samosa for her as a gift - although it seemed brilliant at the time. How hard can it be?

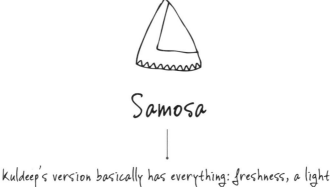

Samosa

Kuldeep's version basically has everything: freshness, a light hint of sweet, just the right heat, and bite.

Any Northern Indian woman can do it... so I decided to try it myself. I make samosa for this Pakistani woman, where I already stand in the kitchen. They are picked up and immediately warmed up in a hot oven. After a serious look of curiosity, tension slowly falls off my shoulders after I see her face lit with a magnificent smile. Mission accomplished!

A samosa is a very popular snack or lunch in Northern India and Pakistan, and by extension in the entire Arab-speaking world as well as Turkey, Goa, Portugal, etc.

The word samosa comes from the Persian *sanbosag* and the first references to this dish are found in the 10th century. The Iranian historian Abolfazl Bayhaqi (995-1075) mentions them in his manuscripts and, with the help of Arab merchants, it became widespread in the 13th and 14th centuries.

Throughout history, a lot has been written about samosa, almost always with praise and appreciation. Amir Khusro, a poet at the court of the Sultan of Delhi, also describes the ingredients in one of his poems: meat,

ghee, onions, almonds, and herbs. The Ain-i-Akbari, an important Mogul gastronomic cultural heritage document from the 16th century, includes the full recipe for qutab, called sanbusah by the Hindi.

This simple restaurant in Southall, the go-to London neighbourhood for typical Indian restaurants, is where you can find, since 1968, phenomenal chicken-stuffed samosa. Kuldeep Singh carries on the tradition and brings a golden triangle, perfectly fried in ghee and with a spice balance to die for. It really must be an innate gift, this spice balance, because even if you closely follow a recipe, the result is rarely what you expected.

A course on balance and complexity. The Bharwa chaat made here is from another planet. Chaat originates in Uttar Pradesh but you can find it all over India. Kuldeep's version basically has everything: freshness, a light hint of sweet, just the right heat, and bite; a really great dish for a ridiculous price.

Here, the essence is clearly in the food and that is how it should be. Impressive!

SPICE VILLAGE

185-189 The Broadway - London UB1 1LX
T +44 20 8574 4475 - http://spicevillageltd.com
Sat.-Thu. 12:00-24:00, Fri. 14:00-24:00

 SOUTHALL

15 minutes by train from Paddington. Leave the station, walk about a hundred yards and you will find yourself in another world. Little India is a fabulous London paradox.

Shahi Haleem

In the treasury that is Indian cuisine, this is truly a crown jewel.

Born after the independence of India in 1947 and grown into a piece of India in London. Obviously, this is the place to be to shop for Indian things and to eat great, authentic Indian food.

Spice Village is one of the classics and certainly one of the nicest restaurants in this dazzling, colourful part of London. Ibrar Khan comes from Lahore; he is very proud of his Pakistani roots. He will share them with you through very typical, local dishes.

I am a very curious gourmet and when I am in a speciality restaurant like this one, I feel like a child in a sweetshop. A speciality from Lahore and a Must Eat by any standard is the Shahi Haleem. At first sight, it looks like a bowl with a sort of sauce. This dish is based on lamb meat, lentils and, of course, spices. The sticky texture and perfect preciseness of the seasoning are truly amazing and addictive. Cooking is so slow and long that the meat almost totally disappears and you only feel it, without seeing it. In the treasury that is Indian cuisine, this is truly a crown jewel.

Also, you can find here the best fish and chips experience you will ever know. The Village famous masala fish is an example for any fish and chips shop, although without the chips. The crust is crispy and also has this spicy touch as if the crust had been caressed by a spicy breeze. Fabulous.

Other hits here undoubtedly include the Charga chicken and a goat leg curry called paya curry.

Hurry and put this restaurant on your To-do list.

ANCHOR AND HOPE

36 The Cut - London SE1 8LP
T +44 20 7928 9898 - www.anchorandhopepub.co.uk

Mon. 17:00-23:00, Tue.-Sat. 11:00-23:00 | lunch 12:00-14:30, dinner 18:00-22:30 | Sun. 12:30-15:15, reservation only

 SOUTHWARK

Anchor and Hope is a genuine British gastropub. The outside of the restaurant doesn't look like much; the inside is plain and very basic, but you feel this patently obvious no-nonsense vibe that you often notice at St. John followers.

*The contents of the plate
is what it's all about.*

Ox Heart, fresh horseradish

Focus and efforts are all centred on the menu: the contents of the plate is what it's all about and that is also what we want as judgement criteria. You don't want guests to go home and dream of the interior décor instead of the food. It seems normal if you are in a restaurant, but we know better. Eating is not necessarily the primary concern in the creation of a winning restaurant concept.

In the beginning, there was only St. John; fortunately, followers have multiplied like rabbits on the fascinating London restaurant scene. Nose to tail ingredients in simple although flavourful combinations, served in a relaxed environment. Anchor and Hope does it to the fullest and for over 10 years has been one of the references for gastropubs in the British capital. No reservations; before dinner, guests mingle in the pleasant bar where beer is served with a hand pump.

The food is simply first-rate thanks to a strict selection of ingredients. Nothing in this matter is left to chance, and compromises are never accepted. It looks like a pub, but the food tastes like in a multi-star temple. That is exactly the definition of a gastropub.

Sometimes, you have to wait a while to get hold of a table, because they do not take reservations, but for this quality of food I will always stand in line.

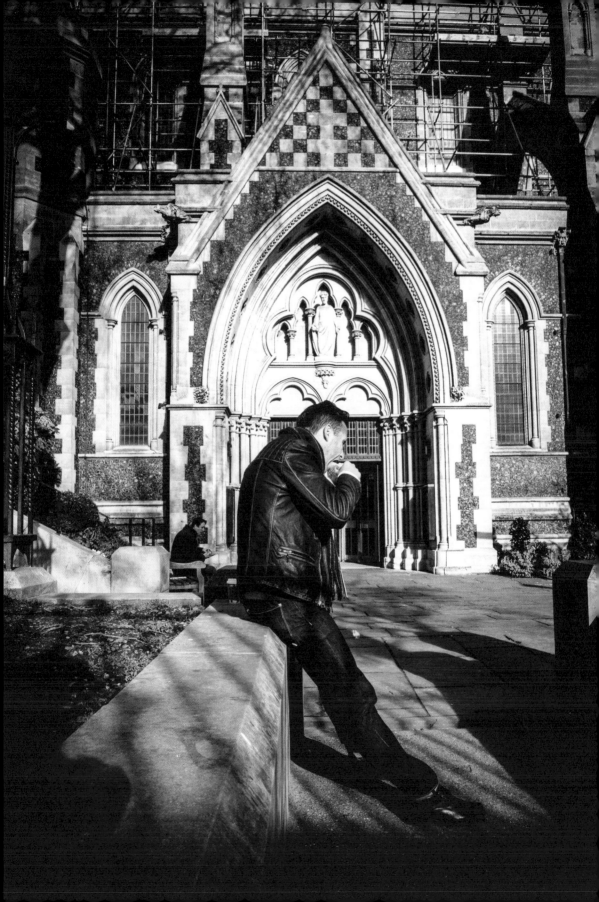

ADDITIONAL EATERIES
SOUTH

A. WONG - £££
70 Wilton Road, Victoria
London SW1V 1DE
T +44 20 7828 8931
www.awong.co.uk
⊖ Victoria
▶ Steamed Duck Yolk Custard

APOLLO BANANA LEAF - £
190 Tooting High Street
London SW17 0SF
T +44 20 8696 1423
⊖ Tooting Broadway
▶ Warmly spiced Crab Masala

LA BARCA - £££
80-81 Lower Marsh
London SE1 7AB
T +44 20 7928 2226
www.labarca-ristorante.com
⊖ Lambeth North
▶ Calamari Fritti

BIBENDUM - ££££
Michelin House, 81 Fulham Road
London SW3 6RD
T +44 20 7581 5817
www.bibendum.co.uk
⊖ South Kensington
▶ Oysters Rockefeller

BOB BOB RICARD - ££££
80-81 Lower Marsh
London SE1 7AB
T +44 20 7928 2226
www.bobbobricard.com
⊖ Oxford Circus
▶ Stinking Bishop Cheese Soufflé

BO LANG - £££
100 Draycott Avenue
London SW3 3AD
T +44 20 7823 7887
www.bolangrestaurant.co.uk
⊖ South Kensington
▶ Dim Sum

CLAUDE'S KITCHEN - £££
51 Parsons Green Lane
London SW6 4JA
T +44 20 7371 8517
www.amusebouchelondon.com
⊖ Parsons Green
▶ Underblade Steak, Date, Earl Grey

THE GOOD LIFE EATERY - ££
59 Sloane Avenue
London SW3 3DH
T +44 20 7052 9388
www.goodlifeeatery.com
⊖ Sloane Square
▶ Healthy Eatery

GRENADIER - ££
18 Wilton Row
London SW1X 7NR
T +44 20 7235 3074
www.taylor-walker.co.uk/pub/grenadier-belgrave-square/c0800/
⊖ Hyde Park Corner
▶ Fish and Chips

HUNAN - ££££
51 Pimlico Road
London SW1W 8NE
T +44 20 7730 5712
www.hunanlondon.com
⊖ Sloane Square
▶ Specialty Tasting Menu

KEN LO'S MEMORIES OF CHINA - £££
65-69 Ebury Street
London SW1W 0NZ
T +44 20 7730 7734
⊖ Victoria
▶ Bang Bang Chicken

MAMA LAN - £££
Unit 18, Brixton Village Market
Coldharbour Lane
London SW9 8PR
www.mamalan.co.uk
⊖ Brixton
▶ Dumplings

MOSIMANNS - ££££
11 West Halkin Street
London SW1X
T +44 20 7235 9625
www.mosimann.com
⊖ Knightsbridge
▶ Cuisine Naturelle

ZAFFERANO - ££££
15 Lowndes Street
London SW1X 9EY
T +44 20 7235 5800
www.atozrestaurants.com/zafferano
⊖ Knightsbridge
▶ Veal Ossobucco Ravioli with Gremolata

GALVIN BISTROT DE LUXE

66 Baker Street - London W1U 7DJ
T +44 20 7935 4007 - www.galvinrestaurants.com/section/4/1/galvin-bistrot-de-luxe
Lunch Mon.-Sat. 12:00-14:30, Sun. 12:00-15:00 I dinner Mon.-Wed. 18:00-22:30, Thu.-Sat. 18:00-23:00, Sun. and holidays 18:00-21:30

 BAKER STREET

A timeless French bistro on Baker Street, the typical London street?
This is what the Galvin Brothers created more than ten years ago.

Lochtartare, potato gazpacho

Inspiration comes straight from the seasonal cuisine of a classic (Southern) French bistro. The interior is lux-urious; service is classy, but the whole experience is rather informal. The dishes radiate class as well as precision. The responsible chef Tom Duffill is clearly not just a chef: he is the best.

The sign on the door says 'Poussez'. And once you push the door, you enter a world that looks totally different from the Baker Street that you left behind. Welcome in the world of French hospitality. You could think you are in Paris, although there, the personnel is often not so inviting or friendly.

Here, under Tom Duffill's guidance, the kitchen's mantra is freshness, uncompromising quality and, if possible, local products. The Galvin brothers have entrusted the kitchen of their flagship restaurant to this dedicated and unassuming chef who sends plate after plate from the kitchen with focused attention.

When you feel that you need to leave London for a moment and go to France, you don't need to take the Chunnel. Here, on Baker Street, any Francophile gourmet will be in seventh heaven for a few hours.

RIVER CAFÉ

Thames Wharf, Rainville Road - London W6 9HA
T +44 20 7386 4200 - http://rivercafe.co.uk
Mon.-Sat. from 12:30 and from 19:00, Sun. from 12:00

 BARONS COURT

Rose Gray and Ruth Rogers have undoubtedly brought something important
to the London restaurant scene. They had a very basic, simple idea that
was innovative and revolutionary.

Chocolate Nemesis

Fresher than fresh ingredients, a menu changed daily, and two chefs behind the stove, who produce their inspiring Italian dishes. In 1987, this was sufficient to establish a legendary restaurant in London.

I would have expected to see this type of restaurant in sun-drenched California cities where fantastic Italian food has been a hit for a long time.

Here, the essence of Italian cuisine is still exposed. To eat at The River Café is like going to a Rolling Stones concert. Yes, the new songs are great, but you primarily came to hear the great classics. And they are great at it: real Italian comfort food that sometimes looks very simple, and it is, but tastes far from simple.

Mind you, the average Italian restaurant customer rarely looks up when he reads the nomenclature on the menu: puntarelle, cima di rape, cicoria, etc. It may look more like a costermonger's barrow in Verona, which indeed is real reassuring for the Italy freak. In any case, The River Café has truly be-come an Italian classic in London.

This place, once a popular neighbourhood restaurant, has indeed grown into a concept. Following the untimely death of one of the founders, Rose Gray, Ruth has enthusiastically carried on. Their cookbooks are on over a million kitchen bookshelves. The rustic cuisine, very simple and straightfor-ward is clearly a staple.

Real Italian comfort food that sometimes looks very simple, and it is, but tastes far from simple.

When my glass is full I empty it,
when it is empty I fill it.

M.J.

HEDONE

301-303 Chiswick High Road - London W4 4HH
T +44 20 8747 0377 - www.hedonerestaurant.com
Thu.-Sat. 12:00-14:30, Tue.-Sat. 18:30-21:30

 CHISWICK PARK

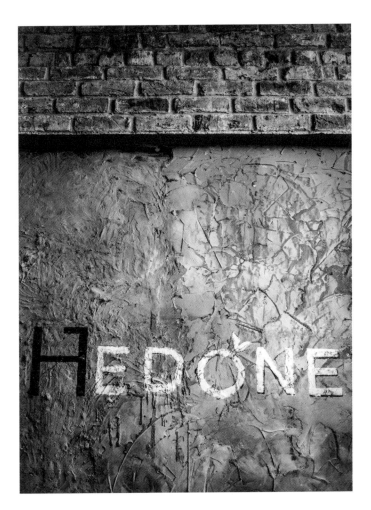

Do you know Gastroville? It was a Swedish food blog specialising in restaurant recommendations and ingredients. It was also linked to a type of consulting, with references of places where you could find the very best ingredients.

Breast and leg of squab pigeon, almond and parsley, paste, smoked potato, black olives, offalsauce

The man behind this is Mikael Jonsson, a lawyer by profession. Generally, bloggers are people who are blamed because they judge and slate restaurants without a lot of practical experience. Well, this Swede has reversed the roles. I'm worried sick that I won't find another blog like his: he has changed course and opened his own restaurant. And what restaurant! Is it the game-keeper who became a poacher, or the other way around?

The cuisine philosophy applied by Jonsson appears somewhat bizarre to people who eat out frequently. Hi is an ingredient freak and would practically give his right arm for the right piece of meat or the right berry. When he finds the perfect ingredient, he will do everything possible to make sure it tastes like it really is. Bizarre, did I say? Or is it the way it should always be?

In a restaurant where ingredients are central, it is of course difficult to maintain high standards. Before opening Hedone, Jonsson spent one year exploring the back of beyond of all shires to discover the best flour, the most flavourful raw butter, or the best fishermen. As a result, his single menu is actually a best of Britain.

To know how good his ingredients really are, all you need to do is sample a few things that you think you know through and through. Take bread, for example. Jonsson took a training course with France's best baker, Alex Croquet. Indeed, the only person who could come and judge the quality of the bread was Croquet himself. The beef comes from high-end butcher Darragh O'Shea: pieces are selected and individually aged for a maximum of 80 days until the texture is a perfect reminder of Japanese beef.

Likewise, the interior is exempt from trinkets and there is a wall of bricks, exposed bricks: bizarre, or logical? Oh yes, there are drawings on the ceiling.

Do not be misled: at Hedone, the plates look as if you would need to assemble them later at home; but the proof of the pudding is in the eating. I had the same feeling when eating at Thomas Keller's. Everything looks almost ridiculously simple, although the depth of flavour and the perfection of taste and combinations will soon convince you that it is actually the contrary.

Great, stunning, Hedone.

RULES

34-35 Maiden Lane - London WC2E 7LB
T +44 20 7836 5314 - www.rules.co.uk

daily from 12:00

 COVENT GARDEN

Thomas Rule promised his family that he would break up with his past and settle in London.
Napoleon had just begun his campaign against Egypt and wanted to take Rule with him,
but the latter declined.

Veal and Morel pie

In 1798, he opened an oyster bar next to Covent Garden. It soon turned out to be a success. In 1998, Rules celebrated its two hundred year existence and it is now the oldest restaurant in London.

This restaurant has had an unbelievably rich history. Charles Dickens, John Galsworthy, Charlie Chaplin, Clark Gable, Stan Laurel, Buster Keaton, HG Wells, and many more shuffled along to enjoy the delicious, very traditional, and amazingly pleasant British cuisine.

Even though the restaurant has changed owner three times, the concept never changed. Right before the Second World War, then owner Charles Rule met Tom Bell, who lived in Paris. Tome had the Alhambra restaurant in Paris, and they simply decided to exchange businesses. At the time, it was that simple.

Eating here is like a memory of long-gone times: it is like dreaming of a fantasy time that we have never known and that will never return. Secretly, I find this type of restaurant fantastic, even more than fantastic. The ritual decanting of a nice bottle of old Bordeaux, or Claret as Englishmen call it, while in the dining room a perfectly aged and prepared partridge is being skilfully sliced. Brilliant! It is such pity that this has become a disappearing restaurant experience.

The partridge was in all likelihood shot on their personal hunting reserve in the High Pennines, the last English wilderness, where all their wild game actually comes from. Classic English cuisine is still a speciality here. Bubbles is the personal 1935 Rolls Royce, property of the restaurant. British monuments together.

A historic meal in a historic setting! This place should receive the World Heritage status.

BUBBLEDOGS

70 Charlotte Street - London W1T 4QG
T +44 20 7637 7770 - www.bubbledogs.co.uk/home
Mon.-Sat. 11:30-16:00, 17:30-23:00

 GOODGE STREET

A champagne bar without caviar, but only with hot dogs? Sometimes, you stumble upon ideas for which you wonder why anyone ever thought of it. Or, maybe he thought of it but why would he be foolish enough to actually act upon it.

Reuben Dog

You have to admit: who doesn't like champagne? And who actually doesn't secretly love hot dogs? Also, the champagnes here are not the great, well-known, trendy brands: these are small, artisanal products.

The Frankfurter is usually known as originating from Frankfurt-am-Main; however, this is contradicted by the fact that the Dachshund (its local name) was made by a butcher from the German city of Coburg, Johann Georg Lahner, somewhere around the end of the 18th century. This butcher went to sell his products in Frankfurt where the sausage became extremely popular. This didn't stop Frank-furt from celebrating the 500th birthday of the hot dog in 1987. In Austria, the Viennese claim the hot dog, called Wiener, was born in their city.

We will never know who is right. And we will never discover who was the first to place a hot dog in the typical bun and sell it as such. It is generally assumed that it was an unnamed German immigrant, who in 1860 had a small food stand in the Bowery in NYC. In 1871, Charles Feltman opened the very first hot dog stand on Coney Island and sold 3684 Dachshund sausages the first year!

Since then, the hot dog has come a long way. Would Bruce Kraig, Ph.D. and retired hot dog historian, know Bubbledogs? James Knappett, the talented Bubbledogs chef who worked in top restaurants such as the Noma and Per Se, adds in my opinion a little hot dog history. In any case, his dogs have this typical, authentic bite and burst that made the hot dog so popular. With his partner Sandia Chang, he created the ultimate restaurant were the hot dog is truly taken seriously.

Whenever I see a Reuben on the menu, I simply can't resist. The Reuben is probably one of the best-known sandwich combos in the United States. Traditionally, it is made of thick slices of corned beef, sauerkraut, sliced cheese, and Thousand Island or Russian dressing. All of this is pressed between two pieces of rye bread and the combination is then toasted. Pure delight!

As is the case with such monumental creations, its origin is controversial. One version says that Reuben Kulakofsky, a Lithuanian grocer from Omaha, Nebraska, invented this sandwich during his weekly poker games with friends in the Blackstone Hotel between 1920 and 1935. The hotel owner and pok-er partner Charles Schimmel put it on his hotel lunch menu and won a national prize with it. Or, does the honour go to Arnold Reuben, the German owner of Reubens Delicatessen, once a well-known deli in NYC? Rumour has it that around 1924 he had a Reuben special on his menu.

I am certain that chef James' experience in NYC is the basis for this nice version of an all time classic, disguised as a hot dog.

Another surprise in this champagne bar and hot dog heaven is the Kitchen Table where calm, intima-cy and focus are keys. Only 19 seats for this no-choice tasting menu in which chef James Knappett throws all his expertise and creativity.

A trendy address offering something for everyone in snazzy Charlotte Street.

DRAKES TABANCO

3 Windmill Street - London W1T 2HY
T +44 20 7637 9388 - www.drakestabanco.com

 GOODGE STREET

A tabanco is a typical tavern from Andalusia, mostly in Jerez de la Frontera, where it is a meeting place for anyone who wants to enjoy a good glass of sherry.

Jamón con oloroso

Here, the sherry nectar is placed on a pedestal and is poured directly from the barrel.

Sherry is an anglicised version of xeres or jerez. The English, who played a very important role in the creation of the complex system of jerez bodega's, first spoke of sack, derived from the Spanish saca, literally tapping wine from the solera. All sherries must originate from the triangle of Jerez de la Frontera, Sanlúcar de Barrameda and El Puerto de Santa María in the Cádiz province. Throughout history, sherry has always had a particular quality status, from the moment the Phenicians introduced wine making into Spain in 1100 B.C. From 200 B.C. on, the Romans took over the torch of wine making. The Moors conquered the area in 711 and introduced distillation. This eventually produced sherry as we know it today: it is a type of stronger wine.

When in 966 the second caliph, Al-Hakam II, ordered the destruction of all vineyards in his caliphate after the full ban of alcohol consumption as a result of the strengthening of religious laws, the inhabitants of Jerez became very creative. Two-thirds of their vineyards were spared because they also delivered delicious grapes to the soldiers.

When Alfonso X of Castille chased the Moors from Jerez in 1264, the sherry boom began and by the end of the 16th century, sherry was considered one of the very best wines in Europe. Colum-bus took sherry with him on his travels to the New World and when Magellan sailed around the world in 1519, he spent more money on sherry than on weapons.

When Francis Drake destroyed most of the Spanish fleet in 1587, he brought 2900 barrels of sherry with him to England. Since then, sherry has been hugely popular here also, and having a glass of sherry is now truly associated with British etiquette and class. When John Cleese asks Lord Melbury what he wants to drink as aperitif and it appears to be a glass of dry sherry, Cleese's only answer is: What else? It says it all; the establishment and their fine manners drink magisterial sherry.

Drakes Tabanco is a small theme park intended to make you believe you are in Andalusia. This type of fantasy is much appreciated by trendy people who enjoy all benefits of living in a large city but still want to step into another world for a while, as if they went to watch a film.

I myself am a sherry fetishist and I'm happy with nice sherry selections in various reincarnations. The tapas are not quite typical of southern Spain, but are rather selected to be the ideal food and wine pairing with the sherry of your choice. For me, the simplest combinations are often the best What is better than a plate of perfectly sliced and aged Iberian ham with a nice glass of oloroso?

What is better than a plate of perfectly sliced and aged Iberian ham with a nice glass of oloroso?

HERMAN ZE GERMAN

43 Charlotte Street, Fitzrovia - London W1T 1RS
T +44 20 7323 9207 - www.hermanzegerman.com
Mon.-Thu. 8:00-23:30, Fri. 8:00-24:00, Sat. 11:00-24:00, Sun. 11:00-22:30

 GOODGE STREET

Do you know the difference between Bockwurst and Bratwurst? The proof of the pudding is in the eating; therefore, I usually order one of each when I come here, simply to refresh my memory and because, of course, both are irresistibly delicious.

Bockwurst
und
Bratwurst

The Bockwurst was invented in 1889 by R. Scholtz, restaurant owner in Berlin. It is one of the most popular German sausage types, and is also much appreciated far outside the German borders. Traditionally, the basis of this speciality is a large portion of finely ground veal meat, filled with a little pork meat. The name explains the origin. This sausage was often eaten with Bockbier, with a generous amount of mustard. This sausage is always poached and sometimes grilled as well.

The Bratwurst, or Brat in American English, is a sausage generally made of veal, pork, and beef. The Old High German word Brät means finely ground meat, or sausage. Many Germans erroneously think that it comes from the verb braten, which actually means to grill or to roast, since today that is exactly what we do. The Bratwurst appeared as soon as 1313 in the German history books, mostly in Franconia.

The reason for opening Herman Ze German was that Azadeh and her German friend Florian could not find the right Bockwurst or Bratwurst in London. In the German Black Forest, Florian's family was one of many generations of butchers. In 2008, they began to import small quantities of sausage and, several food festivals and tastings later, developed a vast group of Wurst fans in London, who come daily to one of their three locations to enjoy this speciality.

The Bockwurst made by butcher Fritz is lightly smoked and tastes the best, in my opinion, in a light, deliciously aromatic, curry sauce. Children and adults alike love it and I myself can happily admit I can't get enough. The pure quality of a hand-made Bockwurst, perfectly seasoned, is simply delicious. The Bratwurst is much more refined and delicate in taste, and I prefer to eat it with a generous tablespoon of mustard.

Herman Ze German is a must-have address and the warm smile of Fräulein Maria is a bonus.

ROKA

37 Charlotte Street - London W1T 1RR
T +44 20 7580 6464 - www.rokarestaurant.com
Mon.-Fri. 12:00-15:30, Sat. 12:30-16:00 | Mon.-Sat. 17:30-23:30, Sun. and holidays 17:30-22:30

🚇 GOODGE STREET

Centuries ago, fishermen from the town of Kushiro, located on Hokkaido,
would sit around a common hearth called the irori.

Kankoku fu kohitsuji
(lamb cutlets with Korean spices)

A red-hot iron was placed in the middle of a sort of sand well and was used as a cooking tool as well as a source of heat and cosiness. Fishermen also took it on board their fishing boats, so that they could cook their food while at sea. To protect the wooden ships from the extreme heat, the glowing binchotan-charcoal was carefully secured in stone casings.

This system has evolved into what we now call the robatayaki, also abbreviated as robata. This method makes it possible to cook food next to the fire, or on top of it. Due to the high quality of the binchotan-charcoal, grilling on a robata is also considered seasoning. The typical flavour of a robata dish is unique.

Roka is a modern version of an authentic robatayaki. The modern architecture firm Super Potato from Tokyo placed the robata grill in a imposing, central location in the restaurant. The fragrance released by the binchotan is delicious and addictive. This charcoal is obtained by steaming hundred years old oak trees for three days at 1200 degrees Celsius, which creates petrified density. As is the case at Zuma, wonder boy Rainer Becker is ultimately responsible for the final version of the dishes. They are served exactly as he likes to eat them: fresh, modern, and flavourful, with sometimes unusual combinations. The courses prepared by experienced robata chefs are truly extraordinary.

For people who would like to discover a less-known aspect of Japanese cuisine, this robata grill is a very pleasant experience for the palate. Before your meal, try a Japan-inspired cocktail based on Shochu in the beautiful lounge in the cellar.

SAKE NO HANA

23 St. James's Street - London SW1A 1HA
T +44 20 7925 8988 - http://sakenohana.com/london
Mon.-Fri. 12:00-15:00, Sat. 12:00-16:00 | Mon.-Thu. 18:00-23:00, Fri.-Sat. 18:00-23:30

Many people don't believe it or can't imagine that, to make perfect sushi you need
10 to 15 years. Sushi has a long history and evolution, and you must be able to taste it.

Sushi —

The simple fish in finger form that lays over a small heap of aromatic rice.

Before being to be taken seriously as a sous-chef in Japan, you must concentrate on it for many years, and only the very best ever reach the status of shokunin. This perfection can be sampled only rarely outside of Japan. Eating sushi should be a fully sensory experience. Everything must be perfect.

An important gastronomic milestone in my life was the tasting of my first top-class sushi. The perfect sushi, as made by Naomichi Yasuda in New York or Jiro Ono in Ginza (Tokyo) is something special and creates an indescribable feel and sensation in your mouth. It is unbelievable that such intensity can be obtained with rice and fish and it illustrates the skill and expertise of a sushi master. It sometimes takes an entire career for a talented, motivated chef to make a sushi that comes close to perfection.

The etymology of the word sushi comes from the ancient Japanese word for sour: suppashi.

Initially, sushi was intended as a conservation method, but it took another two hundred years for the edomae nigiri, the simple fish in finger form that lays over a small heap of aromatic rice, appeared as we know it today. Following an earthquake in 1657, which levelled the city of Edo, there was urgent need for helping and feeding homeless, hungry citizens. The nigiri sushi was thus invented as fast food.

In any event, Hanay Yohei (1799-1858) was the first cook to form small heaps of rice and press, in a fast gesture, fresh raw fish and meat on top of it, hence creating a successful business. His restaurant in Ryogoku, the sumo district in Edo, was the first sushi restaurant in the world.

It would certainly not be the last. In the prestigious St. James' Street, there is a jewel among Japanese restaurants. The inside of this impressive restaurant looks like a futuristic forest, with unbelievable attention for this typical Japanese sense for aesthetics. At the time of opening, Alan Yau was solicited to steer this restaurant in the right direction, and as the perfectionist that he is, he established a very remarkable and addictive restaurant. Sake no Hana is truly a Japanese restaurant that aims to bring something new by maintaining traditional Japanese techniques and preparations of paramount importance.

Hideki Hiwatashi, a well-known chef in Japan, came to London after some convincing to introduce people to the intimacy of his spectacular cuisine. A magnificent Japanese oasis in London.

GREEN PARK   SAKE NO HANA   ££££

193

THE RITZ LONDON

150 Piccadilly - London W1J 9BR
T +44 20 7493 8181 - www.theritzlondon.com

 GREEN PARK

Is there a place where scones with clotted cream and strawberry jam taste better than those of high tea in the Palm Court of the fabulous Ritz Hotel in London?

High tea

A scone is indispensably served with a good high tea.

I will have to remain silent here, because I have never been able to find this beautiful, stylish and typical custom anywhere else.

Anne, Countess of Bedford (1788-1861), is officially the inventor of teatime. Between the earlier frugal midday meal and the very elaborate evening meal, she had a snack every day around 4 in the afternoon. In the beginning, her servants served a few pieces of bread with her tea. However, she began to invite friends for a light, additional meal, with the excuse to drink a cup of afternoon tea. Hence, the Belvoir Castle was the birthplace of the afternoon tea. She kept this habit after returning to London and began sending beautiful official invitations to her friends for this burgeoning social event.

In the second half of the Victorian period, better known as the Industrial Revolution, the term High Tea was born. This name originated from the fact that the average people began to eat rolls, sandwiches, and sometimes also scones and clotted cream at tables of normal height instead of the low salon tables.

A scone is indispensably served with a good high tea. As soon as 1513, there is mention of scones, probably derived from the Dutch 'schoonbrood'. Other sources see it as an adulteration of the Gaelic word sgonn, which means a mouthful. Whatever it is, a scone is and will remain for me one of the typical British items that establish the unbelievable tradition of this country. Along with this other, very typical, British product, the clotted cream, it is food pairing before its time. The monks of Tavistock Abbey were already known for their clotted, clouted, Devonshire or Cornish cream, however you choose to name it. Even more, there are signs that they compensated their workers with a combination of bread, clotted cream, and strawberry jam. So, we know that in the royal Ritz Hotel, the summit of sophistication of the British High Tea used to be a matter of compensation for workers. History has many beautiful twists.

The fastest way for you to feel royal is the Ritz Hotel that opened doors on 24 May 1906. The Piccadilly side of Walsingham House, that used to be part of the Bath Hotel, was converted by hotelier César Ritz into a true institute of world class. For me, it is still the ultimate symbol of British sophistication, etiquette, and elegance. I cannot enter there without a deep sentiment of respect and I always feel tradition flow though my body.

Put on your nicest clothes and make a reservation!

WEST

NOBU

Metropolitan Hotel London, 19 Old Park Lane - London W1K 1LB
T +44 20 7447 4747 - www.noburestaurants.com

Mon.-Fri. 12:00-14:15, Sat.-Sun. 12:30-14:30 | Mon.-Thu. 18:00-22:15, Fri.-Sat. 18:00-23:00, Sun. 18:00-22:00

HYDE PARK CORNER

The first meeting with Nobu included a small Japanese glass, the so-called Uni Shooter.
It is a small shot glass with fresh sea-urchin, some fresh, raw squid,
a raw quail egg yolk, and a little vinaigrette.

Whitefish Sashimi New Style

The idea is to empty the glass in one shot. What a phenomenal explosion of tastes in your mouth. Such mastery certainly reveals a great chef in the kitchen. However, we were sitting in a plain restaurant by a parking lot on La Cienega Boulevard in Los Angeles. I did not know at the time that I was eating with one of the most influential Japanese chefs; one or two hours later, I knew. My table-companion decided, at the end of the meal, to share a last bottle of 1976 Cristal Roederer with the amicable Nobu, and thus created an unforgettable moment in my gastronomic life.

The restaurant was simple; the dishes were not. They revealed a lot of kokoro, as is called in Japan. Dishes with a extra touch from the chef, passion! These are dishes that come straight from the heart.

Nobuyuki Matsuhisa, or Nobu as everyone knows or calls him, is a true phenomenon. When he was seven, his father died in a tragic auto accident. His mother found herself totally alone to feed him and his two brothers. At a very young age, he went to work at Matsue Sushi in Shinjuku where his talent was noticed by a rich Peruvian businessman. In 1973, at the age of 24, Nobu opened a Japanese restaurant, with this man, in Lima. Since he could not find, in Peru, ingredients that he used in Japan, he developed his own style of cuisine through a sort of fusion where Peruvian ingredients were perfectly incorporated in Japanese dishes. A unique style emerged much later, because only now, thirty years later, the crème de la crème of starred chefs see his touch in Peruvian influences.

When in 1987 he opened Matsuhisa in Los Angeles, it naturally, quickly became a hot spot and he became friends with several of his celebrity fans. His friendship with Die Hard star Robert de Niro turned very productive since together they opened their first Nobu in Tribeca, NYC, in 1993. Nobu actually played a few small roles in films, thanks to De Niro, such as in *Memoirs of a Geisha* and in *Casino*.

We had to wait until 1997 before seeing a Nobu in Europe. London was the obvious choice. Christina Ong, owner of Metropolitan, was eager to welcome this Nobu, De Niro, and Drew Nieporent partnership on the first storey of her luxury hotel in Old Park Lane. Since then, Nobu has become one of the trendiest restaurant chains in the world.

Long before others, the visionary character of top chef Nobu has been evident. The exquisite lightness of his magnificent Japanese cuisine, sometimes complemented with subtle Peruvian touches, is sexy and healthy. I always find his cuisine as refreshing as the first time, and the list of favourites here is long: uni tempura, tomato ceviche, baby tiger shrimp tempura with spicy creamy sauce, tea smoked lamb anticucho, miso black cod, whitefish sashimi new style… These are only a few examples of this spectacular repertoire.

The latter is proof of Nobu's art of mixing tradition and innovation. The intense use of koji has only now begun to penetrate the highest gastronomic spheres, whereas his restaurants had been serving it for years to all their clients.

For me, to eat at Nobu is still a moment to which I anxiously look forward.

CAY TRE

42-43 Dean Street - London W1D 4PZ
T +44 20 7317 9118 - http://caytresoho.co.uk/
Mon.-Thu. 11:00-23:00, Fri.-Sat. 11:00-23:30, Sun. 11:00-22:00

LEICESTER SQUARE

A piece of authentic Vietnam in Soho. This is how I can describe this restaurant in a few words.
Here, the process of making Phô (pronounce: feu) takes approximately 18 hours.
The result matches the expectations.

POT-AU-FEU

Phô Bo

When you taste it, you will not miss the depth of the stock.

Phô is a typical dish from Hanoi, more specifically from the province of Nam-Dinh, not far south of this bustling city. It is undoubtedly the number one dish in Vietnam; in Hanoi only, there are more than 300 food stand serving phô portions every day. It is easy to find: just follow the delicious smell of star anise, one of the herbs prominently present in phô.

The two first fixed phô stands in Hanoi still exist today. Cat Tuong in Cau Gô street, and a nameless Chinese kart right by the Bô Ho tram stop. They have been there every day since 1918. Strangely enough, people suppose that the dish was introduced by the French colonizer, sometime between 1870 and 1940. The French ate beef while the Vietnamese ate pork and kept cattle as working animals. The pronunciation 'feu' is probably originating from the French dish 'pot-au-feu'.

Cay Tre is a lot quieter than the average food tent in Hanoi, although it is still very busy. You will never find anything closer to Vietnam's authentic flavours in London. The basic principle here is this: to make the simplest dishes delightful, you have to add passion and time. A good example is the more than 18 hours needed to prepare a bouillon for classic rundphô that has the authentic flavour.

As do a few other Asian cuisines, the Vietnamese strongly believe that balanced nutrition is the key to good health. Their fragrant and hearty phô is a good example of this principle. When you taste it, you will not miss the depth of the stock, no more than the touch of sour, salty, bitter, sweet, and umami; in one word, savouriness. When you eat here, you not only satisfy your stomach: you also please your entire being. A delicious feeling and a happy thought.

RULES OF THE CAFÉ

NO SMOKING
NO FIGHTING
NO CREDIT
NO FOOD FROM OUTSIDE
NO TALKING LOUD
NO SPITTING
NO BARGAINING
NO CHEATING
NO WATER TO OUTSIDERS
NO MATCHES
NO GAMBLING
NO COMBING HAIR
ALL CASTES WELCOME

DISHOOM

12 Upper St. Martin's Lane - London WC2H 9FB
T +44 20 7420 9320 - www.dishoom.com
Mon.-Thu. 08:00-23:00, Fri. 08:00-24:00, Sat. 10:00-24:00, Sun. 10:00-22:00

LEICESTER SQUARE

Old Iranian cafés have almost all disappeared from Bombay. In the beginning of the 20th century, a large number of Iranian immigrants came to Bombay. Of more than 400 cafés that flourished in the Sixties, founded by the followers of prophet Zarathustra, only a handful remains.

Kejriwal

A classic breakfast.

Also, the number of followers of zoroastrianism, an important religion in old Iran, has visibly shrunk: there are probably no more than 100,000 followers remaining.

These typical cafés in the old Bombay, renamed Mumbai, have now practically disappeared from the street scene, much to the discontent to many a Bombayites. One of the oldest that is still open is Merwan café, established in 1914. They were meeting places for rich businessmen, sweaty taxi wallas, and loving couples. Students had breakfast here, families had dinner, solicitors read their documents, and writers discovered their main characters. Here, under a slow-turning fan, where Bentwood chairs reflected in the spotted mirrors and sepia family portraits covered the walls, here is what everything happened in Bombay.

Dishoom Café is an ode to this typical Bombay phenomenon. The interior is fun, cosy, with that perfect little vintage touch. The menu is fusion, from a period when fusion was still called colonialism. In all Bombay cafés, you could see photos of muscular Iranian wrestlers who thought their powerful bundle of muscles was the result of eating a hearty breakfast.

For me, a classic is the kejriwal, not to be confused with the famous Indian politician, Arvind Kejriwal. Kejriwal is a classic breakfast dish in the prestigious Willingdon Sports Club in Bombay. This institution, founded in 1918 by Lord Willingdon, is undoubtedly the most prestigious golf club in Mumbai. It happened to be the first club in India where locals were allowed to become members. Over the last thirty years, no entirely new member has been admitted, and new members are only first-degree relatives of people who are already members. In this club, kejriwal is a hit. It may have been invented here, after one man kept ordering a strange breakfast dish. He ordered toast with cheese, spring onion, chilli, and fried eggs. This man's name was Kejriwal and he was a Marwari, a strictly vegetarian ethnic group. However, his love for eggs was greater than his conviction and since these delicacies were irrevocably a total and clear no-go at home, he went to his favourite club to order a mixture of cheese, chilli and spring onion baked on a toast, then covered with two delicious fried eggs.

Even though I am not an Iranian wrestler, whose photograph hangs in the Yazdani Café, I tended to combine with the almost as delicious qeema per eedu, where nicely seasoned minced chicken and chicken liver are baked with a fried egg and crispy chips.

Also, try a dhoble, a breakfast cocktail, and you will have a fine day.

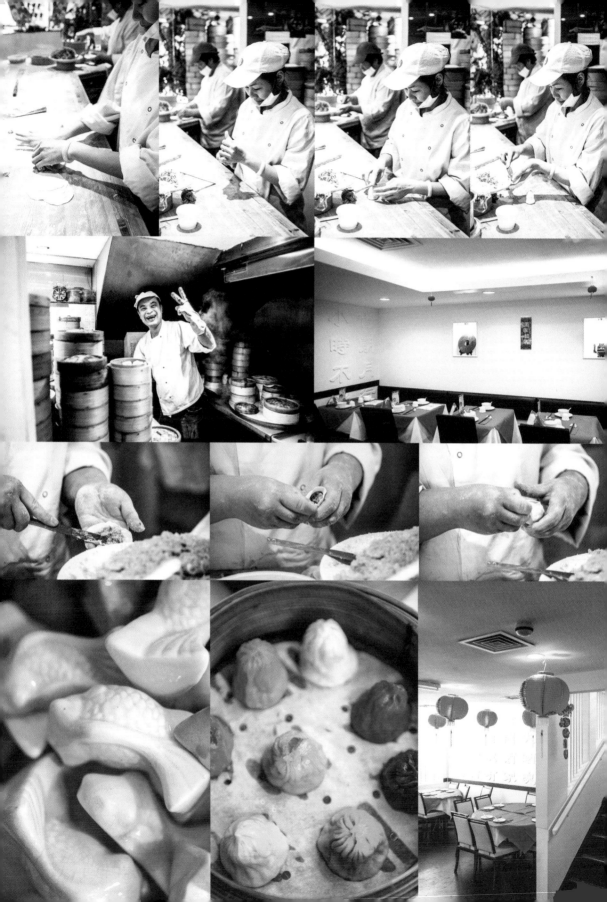

DUMPLINGS' LEGEND

6 Gerrard Street - London W1D 6JE
T +44 20 7494 1200 - www.dumplingslegend.com
Mon.-Thu. 12:00-24:00, Fri.-Sat. 12:00-03:00, Sun. 12:00-23:00

LEICESTER SQUARE

There is not much left of the original Chinatown that spontaneously grew in the eastern part of London in the beginning of the 20th century. The current Chinatown that developed next to Shaftesbury Avenue in the late sixties is now the beating heart of the Chinese community in London.

Xiao long bao

Dumplings made of a thin, steamed dough pouch filled with a small ball of aromatic ground meat and a hearty, liquid bouillon.

In the main street of Chinatown, music history was also written. In August 1968, in Gerrard Street, people heard from the very first time the sounds of 'Train Kept a Rollin' by a group having its first rehearsal and chose the name Led Zeppelin.

Dumplings' Legend puts a stop to the idea that the kitchens of Chinese restaurants in Chinatown are always dirty and grubby. It is actually an open kitchen where you can see dim sum chefs busy doing their thing. Here, the speciality is, in my opinion, the famous Xiao long bao. The mysterious dumpling was made of a thin, steamed dough pouch filled with a small ball of aromatic ground meat and a hearty, liquid bouillon. I still wonder how they do it.

Xiao long bao is a steamed dim sum, a baozi from Shanghai or Wuxi. Traditionally, it is served in a xian long or typical bamboo basket in which it is steamed. This is where it gets its name. We see this well-known dim sum first appear in Nanxiang, a neighbourhood of Shanghai in the Jiading District. The inventor if Xiao long bao was selling them in his shop in Nanxiang next to

the Guyi Garden entry, the most well-known park of the city. From there, this hearty dim sum gained popularity and conquered the city centre.

The original shop is still in business but has been moved. The traditional Nanxiang Mantou Dian is now located by this other beautiful park, the Yu Garden. The second traditional Xiao Long bao restaurant is called Guyipark; it took over the original Nanxiang site at the Guyi park.

In addition to being unbelievably delicious and hearty, Xiao long bao is also very pretty and aesthetic. The dough is left to rise only partially, which, when steamed, gives it a very transparent and soft skin. The dough is turned and pinched shut on the upper side, which prevents gelatinised bouillon from coming out.

At Legend, they master this technique particularly well. In addition, they offer a wide choice of delicious dim sums. Use caution when you enthusiastically taste this fabulous Xiao long bao: you could burn your tongue because the stock is really very hot.

LA GELATIERA

27 New Row - London, Covent Garden WC2N 4LA
T +44 20 7836 9559 - www.lagelatiera.co.uk
Mon. 10:00-23:00, Wed.-Sat. 10:00-23:30, Sun. 11:00-23:00

LEICESTER SQUARE

Ice cream is still cool, literally and figuratively. Antonio lived in Calabria where his grandfather was a well-known ice cream maker.

Basil and chilli gelato

Raw milk from Jersey cows is delivered daily to guarantee the freshness.

This tradition is carried on in Soho and all ice cream is made daily with only fresh ingredients and organic dairy products. A gelatiera is the name of a traditional ice cream churn used by artisanal ice cream makers. There are no secrets: their work place and lab are open to anyone interested.

Here, you can see for yourself how serious ice cream making can be. Raw milk from Jersey cows is delivered daily to guarantee the freshness. All flavours are made on site, with fresh ingredients and in small quantities, which also ensures freshness and taste. The traditional Mantecazione process is still applied as before. No additives anywhere! The work here is done based on the core of the slow food concept.

Ice cream has of course travelled a long journey in history. The Romans are known to have mixed snow with flavours such as honey and fruit; however, the origin of ice cream as we know it today goes back to various very rich European royal houses. Indeed, for centuries, ice cream was a delicacy that only the super-rich could afford. Alexander the Great (356-323 B.C.) used to send slaves into the mountains to collect ice, and Nero made his slaves gather snow n the mountains to serve it with honey and fruit during is decadent banquets. However, it would be the Chinese who chilled a mixture of milk, flour and camphor in a metal tube in snow, thus making the very first ice cream.

Ice cream progress got out of hand when Catharina de Medici married the French King Henri II in 1533 and brought her ice from Italy. From then on, the popularity of ice cream spread as fire through European noble and royal houses.

Sicilian Procopio dei Coltelli was the first to introduce the average people to the magical, refreshing treat when he opened Le Procope in Paris in 1686, the very first ice cream parlour in the world. Benjamin Franklin and Victor Hugo were regulars there to lick and spoon the frozen mixture of milk, cream, eggs, and butter at the house of the father of ice cream.

Some flavour combinations at La Gelatiera are at the very least original: Porcini and chocolate, Cor-nish blue cheese and walnuts, Alphonso mango, Peach Bellini, honey, rosemary and zest, and of course the fabulous basil and chilli that create a true explosion in the mouth, although in total bal-ance.

Look no further: you have found the best ice cream in London.

GOODMAN

24-26 Maddox Street - London W1S 1QH
T +44 20 7499 3776 - www.goodmanrestaurants.com

Mon.-Sat. 12:00-22:30 (last order)

 OXFORD CIRCUS

In the Lascaux caves, you can admire drawings showing that people hunted bovine.
This means that eating beef is almost as old as man is. Around 8000 B.C., man began to
domesticate cattle so as to have immediate and daily access to milk, leather, and meat.

Ribeye

Beef is the third most eaten meat in the world. With 25%, it only comes after poultry (30%) and pork (38%). Argentinians are by far the largest beef consumers with 64kg per capita annually. When man actually began baking or roasting beef is not know with certainty. Some breeds were raised in the old world for milk or meat, and with the progress in farming mechanisation, breeds such as chianina and charolais were intensively raised to maximise meat yield, while angus, for example, was raised for the finer texture of its meat.

When I stand in front of a display of pieces of beef that all look close to perfection, I understand peo-ple who stand in awe in front of a window with exclusive watches. In this carnivore peep show, I no-tice several pieces on which I almost hallucinate to see my name stamped on them. Goodman is a meat lovers paradise, you already understood. I strongly suspect that Goodman has been declared a vege-tarian-free zone.

The classic layout and feel evokes a typical Manhattan steakhouse where music is just a little too loud because people shout a little too loud, or is it the contrary? Is the idea of directly eating a seri-ous piece of perfectly cooked dead cow enough to reactivate the primal hunter instinct in us? It may be that we even feel the primitive man resurging in us, but we still leave our bow and arrow at the door.

In this restaurant, attended by many regulars, you will recognize the super regulars by their very own steak knife, carved with their initials. Talk about a hunting trophy! In my opinion, this place ranks in the top 5 of the very best steak experiences ever. I have eaten monumental steaks at Satou in Tokyo, Peter Luger in Brooklyn, Casa Julian in Tolosa, and here. For me, the ultimate steak experience is still La Table du Boucher in Mons, Belgium, where cow whisperer Luc Broutard has develop such mastery in ageing beef that it has become an art followed by many.

At Goodman's the quality of the meat is clearly impressive. They specialise in ageing corn-fed angus from the American Lake District with a texture that usually is a little sweet and very fine, and the heavier, wilder-tasting local British breeds.

Übung macht den Meister. When you bake or grill large quantities of steaks of all sorts of different cuts, you naturally become an expert in the field. Hence, chef Phil succeeds in offering perfect steaks: steaks with impeccable and correct colour, smell, and texture. Not much is needed to satisfy the primitive hunter: a perfect (Flintstone size) steak is largely sufficient.

You will recognize the super regulars by their very own steak knife, carved with their initials.

E OF US VALUED FOOD.
& SONG, ABOVE HOARDING GOLD.
ULD BE A MERRIER WORLD" J.R.R. TOLKIEN

CHIMEK 치맥

I CAN'T KEEP CALM I'M KOREAN

I ♥ K-POP

50000

珍珠 진주

JINJUU

15 Kingly Street - London W1B 5PS
T +44 20 8181 8887 - http://jinjuu.com/
Mon.-Sat. 12:00-15:00 and 18:00-24:00, Sun. 12:00-16:00

⊖ OXFORD CIRCUS

Korea, or Uri-nara, its Korean name, is a country of very rich gastronomic culture. As a matter of fact, the Western name Korea is an evolutive declension of the tenth century dynasty, Goryeo.

Korean fried chicken

The Dutchman Hendrick Hamel (1630-1692) was a shipwrecked sailor who lived in Korea for thirteen years and introduced the spelling 'Korea' to our world. In the South, Koreans call their country Han-Guk; South Koreans call North Korea Buk Han and when speaking of their own country, they say Joseon. Both peoples also use the name Uri Nara, which means our country.

Regarding gastronomy, Korea is a country that has a lot to offer; however, you will find very few Korean restaurants that are worth the name. And when you find one, you will often be served an insipid decoction of gogigui or Korean barbecue. It is a pity, because as is often the case, what is unknown is unloved.

Korea's national dish is and of course remains kimchee. Even so that, when Koreans are asked to smile, for instance for a photograph, they usually say kimchee, as we say cheese. Kimchee is greater than Korea because it is one of the oldest recipes of vegetables that are pickled, fermented, and soaked in brine. It is mentioned in *Xin Nan Shan* poems from the seventeenth century. There are officially 187 kimchee versions but in practice there are probably as many kimchee recipes as there are kimchee cooks.

The eating culture reflects Korean life philosophy. The pursuit of yin & yang: warm, cold, mild and hot... and explosion of flavours, fragrances, and textures. Culinary sensations in which the primary accent is on simplicity.

Korean cuisine could not find a better ambassador than Judy Joo. She hosts several TV programmes in the UK and in the United States highlighting Korean cuisine. Her enthusiasm for her Korean cuisine is utterly contagious.

She is a genuine Jinjuu, the Korean word for pearl, also the name of her first restaurant in London where she introduces her critical guests to her modern approach of traditional Korean cuisine. In the trendy Carnaby Street borough, she runs her business on two levels. The theme of the lower floor is anju, the type of appetizers often accompanying a drink. Among them, the fantastic and utterly addictive Korean fried chicken steals the show, together with the Bulgogi style burgers and the delicious, hearty dumplings; on the other floor, a more complete experience awaits you.

Even though Judy is no celebrity chef, she is well known by the general public. She carries out her mission, namely to introduce Korean cuisine to the general public, with deep fervour. This should not be too difficult with the food served here: it is a pure delight!

NOPI

21-22 Warwick Street - London W1B 5NE
T +44 20 7494 9584 - www.ottolenghi.co.uk/locations
Mon.-Fri. 08:00-14:45 and 17:30-22:30, Sat. 10:00-11:30, 12:00-22:30, Sun.10:00-16:00

OXFORD CIRCUS

Yotam Ottolenghi was born in Jerusalem from an unusual mix: an Italian father and a German mother. He grew up in the multicultural Ramat Denya neighbourhood of this large city.

Roasted aubergine, black garlic, chilli, broad beans, basil

When he came to live in London in 1997, although he wanted to obtain a PhD, he also enrolled in the well-known cooking school of Le Train Bleu. This is where his unmistakable talent quickly came to light.

Since then, his cooking style has evolved but his dishes remain strongly rooted in the Middle East. The nice thing, however, is that they are not locked in this straitjacket. His great talent lies in the inimitable combination of his Israeli cuisine with a wide spectrum of flavours and textures found in the entire Mediterranean region, the Middle East, and part of Asia. Syrian, Lebanese, Iranian, and Armenian flavours are house-made and used as paint for his gorgeous paintings.

His signature dishes are beautifully interlaced flavours that make you dream of the Middle East. Many people are probably too happy to dream away to the Middle East through the mysterious, distinct tastes of Ottolenghi, because his cookbooks are best sellers all over the world. And indeed, I actually see them displayed in every library.

In 2002, he opened his first deli restaurant in Notting Hill. It was a success. Nopi was established in 2011 and is a deli that is more focused on restaurant service; we call it a gourmet deli. The place is light and joyful and the flavours are more than ever colourful and exciting! I am definitely impressed by his vegetarian dishes that look irresistible and taste even better.

WEST

PITT CUE CO

1 Newburgh Street - London W1F 7RB
T +44 20 7287 5578

Mon.-Sat. 12:00-15:00, 17:30-23:00, Sun. 12:00-16:00

 OXFORD CIRCUS

In Soho, very close to the ever world-famous Carnaby Street,
is a small jewel tucked in a corner.

Caramel Ribs

It is a very small restaurant in which great numbers of people want to enter to try the fabulous barbecue art of this top team.

As an answer to the on-going crisis, two friends, Jamie Berger and Tom Adams, decided to bring their version of the beloved American BBQ to the London street food scene. They started on a parking lot under Hungerford Bridge and quickly became a trend via social media, creating a rush for their riblets. This success almost forced them to exchange the food stall for a permanent location.

No reservations! Not in the small bar on the ground floor, and not in the pocket restaurant in the basement. The concept is simple and takes the space limitations into account. They focus on four or five items, which they do amazingly well. The food is so good that you will sometimes wait for a ridiculous period of time, and with pleasure. This is truly a restaurant where the eating experience is devoid of any useless weight. Pitt Cue can only accommodate two services of 30 hungry customers per evening. So, keep in mind that you will probably have to stand in line for a while, sometimes outside and sometimes in the small, crammed bar. The good news is that in the bar you can taste a small portion of their signature ribs.

The menu changes daily; it is nicely written on a board and just by reading it, you will awaken the hungry dog in you. Do not underestimate this little address. Their own interpretation of the southern USA BBQ is actually refined and to the point.

Phenomenal.

YAUATCHA

15-17 Broadwick Street - London W1F ODL
T +44 20 7494 8888 - www.yauatcha.com
Mon.-Sat. 12:00-23:30, Sun.12:00-22:30, patisserie counter: 12:00-23:00

 OXFORD CIRCUS

Dim ergo sum. Dim sum is undoubtedly my favourite way of eating. I am always highly impressed by the speed at which true dim sum restaurants can bring to my table an unbelievable variety of tastes and shapes. Everyone samples and enjoys: it is truly pleasant and fun for everybody.

Siu mai

Contrary to what many people wrongly believe, dim sum is not a specific appetizer. It is a manner of eating. Dim sum literally means 'trouble the heart' although in very ancient manuscripts, it is also a sort of verb meaning 'to eat something small'. In Cantonese, one talks of yum cha, which actually means 'to drink tea'. This better explains the origin of dim sum. It comes from the Silk Road era when many resting places were created for the many travellers: tea was served, accompanied by small bites. In Mandarin Chinese, dim sum is called dian xin. It was mostly popular in Guangzhou; the phenomenon later spread all over China, to Hong Kong where it is now more popular than ever. In very large cities, you will still find these typical mega dim sum restaurants where, after the banning of opium rooms you could play mahjong to your heart's content while they drove by in steam karts.

Of course, everything is prepared by hand, only when the client places an order. The dim sum chefs are quick and skilled. My all-time favourite is the siu mai. I eat it in every dim sum in which I enter, and is sort of a benchmark for each dim sum chef. I think everyone actually knows it. The genuine, original siu mai first appeared in inland Mongolia, specifically in Hohhot, sometime between the Ming and the Qing dynasties. The name siu mai means something like 'making and selling quickly'. It was so popular that it was rolled, steamed, and sold immediately.

How Alan Yau does it, I don't know; but the dim sums in his Yauatcha taste better than in the most traditional places in, say, Hong Kong. The precision and inspiration of his executive chef Tong, who knows how to bring out the best in everyone, is almost legendary, and so are his dim sum creations. At Yauatcha, you will return to the original roots of the dim sum cuisine. They are served with tea. In addition to a nice wine list, you will also find a very rich tea menu. Yau has also allowed pastry chef Graham Hornigold to express his diabolic talents so as to offer a varied and hugely attractive patisserie corner. No matter how good Graham is with his passion, dim sum is the magic word here.

At Yauatcha, you will return to the original roots of the dim sum cuisine.

BABAJI PIDE

53 Shaftesbury Avenue, Soho - London W1D 6LB
T +44 20 3327 3888 - www.babaji.com.tr
Mon.-Thu. 12:00-23:00, Fri.-Sat. 12:00-23:30, Sun. 12:00-22:00

 PICCADILLY CIRCUS

When Alan Yau, in my opinion the most respected entrepreneur in the hotel and catering
industry in the world, takes on something, he doesn't leave anything to chance.

Pide

The pide universe is much wider than it looks at first.

It in in this spirit that he opened this modern Turkish pide restaurant, because he had been disappointed so many times when sampling pide, whether in London or, for instance, in Istanbul. It seemed as if the pride in making this staple of Turkish gastronomic cultural heritage had disappeared in everyone. Nonetheless, Yau noticed that the potential of a good, flavourful pide is huge.

Even in Istanbul, the best pide salonu is only 50 years old; so, Yau decided it was time for pide to also conquer London. Babaji is his answer!

The word babaji, spelled babaci in Turkish but pronounced babaji, expresses the affection that a son or daughter has for his/her father. In addition, the repetition of the letter a gives a sort of verbal rhythm that is highly positive and pleasant.

Etymologically, it is generally assumed that the word pide comes from the Greek pitta; the Italians are believed to have translated the same word into pizza. At first sight, a pide looks very basic. It appears as boat-shaped flat bread where the hull is used to carry the various toppings from the stone oven to the table. However, after only a few trips to Turkey, it quickly becomes clear that the pide universe is much wider than it looks at first.

Yau searched for, and found his kitchen staff in the Tarlabasi neighbourhood in Istanbul. Ali and Ahmet, two brothers from the town of Develi in Kayseri, have made pide during their entire lives. They both left for the big city at a very young age to pursue their dream. There, they opened the well-renowned Develi Pide salonu. They work in perfect symbiosis: Ahmet treats the noble pieces of beef with surgical precision while Ali takes care of the dough and keeps the fire burning with blocks of charcoal and the occasional broken chair. These people get it: they work with focus, pleasure, and respect. They are the third generation of pideci who made the patented civikli pide mostly in Develi.

The kitchen of Babaji is in their expert hands.

As soon as you have stepped over the threshold of Babaji, your quest for the perfect pide is over.

DUCKSOUP

41 Dean Street - London W1D 4PY
T +44 20 7287 4599 - www.ducksoupsoho.co.uk
Open daily 12:00-15:00 and 18:00-23:00

Ⓤ PICCADILLY CIRCUS

Next to this restaurant is the Groucho Club. For people who live on another planet,
Groucho is one of the legendary Marx Brothers who created the anarchistic and
legendary comedy called *Duck Soup*.

Deep fried artichokes, blood orange, almond aïoli

Clare Lattin, Rory McCoy and chef Julian Biggs found Ducksoup to be a fitting name for their project. Could it be that their vinyl collector's mania absolutely has anything to do with it? Indeed, in this small restaurant, they are mad about vinyl, and whenever I hear Red Red Wine by the group named as an unemployment form, I cannot help but think back to the tie when I ripped this album out of its packaging and put it on my record-player. Such collective memories create bonds even if we didn't know this about each other. People who still have some vinyls at home but like me do not have a record-player, can bring their favourite album here and play it: a sort of corkage for music.

Some restaurants swear by local, others prefer to go for international inspiration and benefit from the amazing logistic opportunities offered by a city such as London in terms of offerings of top quality products from the entire world. Here, travels are an inspiration source for the dishes. These are dishes that are the choice of the moment or that are linked to a trip. They must be simple, so that the ingredients or idea can remain central. Simple cuisine with delicious flavours.

Ducksoup does offer true local flair: it is small and cosy, and its décor is not spectacular. However, the food is spectacular. This restaurant operates kind of like a soup where ingredients influence each other. A little Brit, a touch of Mediterranean, a hint of Scandinavia and quite a bit of Middle East; if possible, still some Asian. That is Ducksoup, and this mix creates a very good modern restaurant.

MINAMOTO KITCHOAN

44 Piccadilly - London W1J 0DS UK
T +44 207 437 3135 - www.kitchoan.com
Mon.-Fri. 10:00-19:00, Sat. 10:00-20:00

PICCADILLY CIRCUS

Japanese cuisine and Japanese influences in our Western gastronomy have never been so great. However, there is at least one aspect of the ingenious and subtle Japanese cuisine that has not penetrated the West in any way: it is the wagashi.

Oribenishiki   kurishigure

Both creations emphasize the best of the chestnut flavour.

Wagashi is a traditional pastry form of Japan, usually served with tea. Milk or eggs are never used; the most frequent basic ingredients are ancho (pasta made of azuki or red beans), mochi, and fruit.

The preparation of sweet dishes by adding isolated sugars is not traditional in the old Japan: this is clearly shown in the old word for sweets, okashi, that always refers to nuts and fruit. It is not until the end of the Muromachi period (1337-1573), with the emergence of travel to traditional tea houses and apparition of dim sum, that some wise men and philosophers brought this recipe from China. I also name wagashi the best sweet dim sum. This rich cultural part of Japanese history, during which, among others, the beautiful golden temple in Kyoto, the Kinkaku-ji, was built, is also characterised by an international burst of Japanese commercial relationships.

Since 1543, Portuguese merchants came periodically to do business; so did the Spaniards starting in 1587, and the Dutch from 1609. However, at the time, the Japanese dessert art was not appreciated by these Western traders who saw commerce everywhere.

The noble art of the wagashi flourished in Japan in the following period, the so-called Edo period (24 March 1603-3 May 1868). Under one of the most iconic shoguns, Tokugawa Ieyasu, brought stability and calm in Japan, thus also a time in which their noble culture could prosper.

Wagashi exists in all flavours and colours, but is always seasonal. I mostly anticipate chestnut season: this nut is very appreciated in Japan. If the offering of a large company such as Minamoto Kitchoan, includes of course, seasonal products, I resolutely choose oribenishiki and kurishigure. Both creations emphasize the best of the chestnut flavour. As is the case with many preparations of Japanese cuisine, the main ingredient is always the most important. Chestnut: puréed, candied or otherwise treated; a very small amount of unrefined sugar such as wasanbon; and rice to give texture. Nothing more is necessary to be blown away by the power of simplicity.

Wagashi always looks beautiful: a paragon of aesthetic perfection: only the Japanese have it as innate quality.

This shop has eight modest tables. When you enter her from busy Piccadilly and hear the beautiful sound of Japanese bamboo flute, sit down with a bowl of freshly brewed matcha and indulge in a wagashi (insanely good with matcha). Suddenly, life looks very different. This is one of my favourite places for relaxing in London.

ABU ZAAD

29 Uxbridge Road - London W12 8LH
T +44 20 8749 5107 - www.abuzaad.co.uk

SHEPHERD'S BUSH MARKET

There is only a handful Syrian restaurants in London; among them, Abu Zaad is probably the most authentic. Syrian cuisine is surprisingly unknown and much underestimated.

Farrouj Abu Zaad

A complex preparation of delicately marinated chicken sliced horizontally and grilled on charcoal.

Syria has a very peculiar geographic location, with borders with Turkey, Lebanon, Israel, Jordan, and the Mediterranean Sea. Additionally, the Euphrates River runs through this country. Therefore, it is in the middle of one of the world's most culturally sophisticated areas, including in terms of gastronomy. As a result of a diaspora of civilisations, their cuisine has become what it is today: one of the cradles of what we name, for the sake of convenience, Mediterranean cuisine.

Apart from a few differences, Syrian cuisine and eating habits are fairly similar to the Lebanese cuisine. Dishes are mostly served in the form of a mezze. Syrian cuisine has always been transmitted from mother to daughter; consequently, tradition says alive and recipes barely change.

The Farrouj Abu Zaad is an inimitable dish. It is a complex preparation of delicately marinated chicken sliced horizontally and grilled on charcoal to succulent but crisp perfection. It is and remains a surprisingly flavourful cuisine, at a great price/quality ratio.

Every day, the place is full of teens, young families and couples who evidently placed this nice Syrian restaurant high on their list. As is customary in a neighbourhood restaurant, portions are huge and the atmosphere is always busy and pleasant. Fortunately, you never have to wait very long for a table.

Damascus is considered one of the oldest cities in the world that has always been inhabited. According to historians, the roots of Damascus go as far as 7000 B.C. and the city has always been a civilisation melting pot. At Abu Zaad, you have the opportunity to discover a sample of Syrian hospitality. A delightful address, to keep and cherish.

CHOTTO MATTE

11-13 Frith Street - London W1D 4RB
T +44 20 7042 7171 - www.chotto-matte.com
Mon.-Sat. 12:00-01:30, Sun. 13:00-24:00

TOTTENHAM COURT ROAD

It had to happen! Finally, a restaurant where the love affair between Japanese
and Peruvian cuisines is publicly displayed.

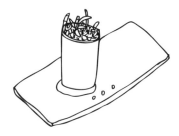

Seabass Ceviche

Nobu has been doing it for many years, but doesn't advertise it in such a manner. While at Nobu, the Peruvian influences are somewhat restrained, Kurt Zdesar makes no secret of this.

The three-story Chotto Matte intends to capture the energy from Tokyo's avant-garde underground scene by serving the so-called Nikkei cuisine. Zdesar came to know it in 1996 at Nobu and totally fell under its spell. In Peter Gordon, whom the night zappers among us may still know as jury member in Master Chef New Zealand, he found a partner in crime in the love for Nikkei food.

Actually, Nikkei originates from Peru, where the second greatest Japanese community in South America lives and works. There is a large presence of Nikkei chefs and restaurants, mostly in Lima. Therefore, it is no coincidence that the haute couture of the culinary world flocks over there to find inspiration, and I'm being polite here. Nikkei is not new: it was born almost one hundred years ago when restaurants began to combine their Japanese clients' love for fresh fish with yucca, potatoes, aji peppers, and corn.

When in 2004 Zdesar stopped by Nobu, he had travelled extensively and was mentally focused on opening, one day, a Nikkei restaurant. He scoured Peruvian restaurants all over the world.

In Lima, he was mostly impressed by Central, in the Miraflores neighbourhood. He also notices that this cuisine has now conquered the entire culinary world, while all it does is combining vegetables and fruit from the Amazon region, that most people have never seen, with purely Japanese elements. This also happens in many restaurants in Shanghai, California, and Amsterdam.

The genuine Nikkei cuisine was here intentionally somewhat subsided because the Western palate is not ready for this potent, powerful combinations with a lot of lime, chilli, raw onion, and fish sauce. Here, dishes are highly balanced while remaining explosive.

I do have a soft spot for this Japanese food with a South American twist. Anyhow, Chotto Matte is a standard Japanese expression for 'wait a moment'. I feel that Nikkei cuisine has waited a long time before quietly charming the culinary world. Certainly now that the Adria brothers have opened their own Nikkei restaurant in Barcelona, named Pakta.

Zdesar is certainly in close touch with this spirit of the time of culinary pulse; Nikkei cuisine is so delicious, flavourful, colourful, light, and healthy, that it has a great future ahead.

WEST

HAKKASAN

8 Hanway Place - London W1T 1HD
T +44 20 7927 7000 - www.hakkasan.com

 TOTTENHAM COURT ROAD

What do you say when words are not enough? That sentence haunted my head when
I tried to describe Hakkasan in a way that didn't appear as if I owned a whole lot of
shares of the company.

Peking duck with Qiandao caviar

What is the most perfect restaurant in the world? This is a question often answered without being asked, in countless lists and scores that people keep harping on about year after year. For me, this question has had only one answer since 2001: Hakkasan Hanway Place. I must have eaten there more than ten times even though I don't live exactly around the corner, and I have recommended the place to hundreds of people.

Very close to busy Tottenham Court Circus is a small, narrow alley: this gastronomic nirvana is located 20 metres underground, where the feel good factor is unequalled and where all worries of the real world are pushed far away. It is an oasis.

Who could have predicted that a certain Alan Yau, born in 1962 in Sha Tau Kok, would grow to be one of the most brilliant restaurant entrepreneurs in the world? Moreover, he would once and for all put the delicacy and pure essence of the rich Chinese cuisine on the world map. In his Hakkasan, every-thing fits.

When you descend the monumental staircase and swing open the dark doors, you enter another world; a world where everything is nicer and better. The famed designer Christian Liaigre created here Yau's perfect vision by finding inspiration in a detailed description, in a novel, of the interior of a chic bar in 1930 Shanghai. Subdued colour combinations and rich materials create a unique ambiance oscillating between mystery and decadence. The chefs' movements are visible only through their backlit silhouettes and the matte partition openings add dimension to the restaurant's theatre. In this Feng Shui space, you never have the impression of being in a windowless restaurant, thanks to simple lighting techniques and unique spatial perception.

The culinary magician who could create the gastronomic part of Yau's ideas was the highly talented Tong Chee Hwee, Hakkasan executive chef since opening day. He came from the kitchen of the Summer Pavilion, the well-known restaurant of the Ritz-Carlton in Singapore.

I could elaborate forever over the attention to detail in preparation and service, the atmosphere, the franchising concept and other locations; for me, Hakkasan is inextricably bound to this first location where everything began. Of course, most important is the plate: what is placed on it is simply phenomenal. Here, you could blindly choose any 'must eat', because everything is top class. The jasmine tea smoked chicken is a staple, and the dim sums are a must; however, as an unconditional lover of caviar, I choose the Peking duck with Qiandao caviar without hesitation. This dish is truly an unforgettable experience in terms of texture as well as aromas; many great chefs have felt a call to prepare it but never fully succeeded. Fortunately, you do not have to select one dish; you can browse the menu to your heart's content.

The only question I always ask myself at Hakkasan is when will I return? It is a pity I don't live close by.

KOYA

49 Frith Street - London W1D 45g
T +44 20 7434 4463 - www.koya.co.uk
Mon.-Sun. 12:00-15:00, 17:30-22:30, Sun. 22:00

TOTTENHAM COURT ROAD

Since Michelin also makes culinary guides in Japan and amazes friend and foe with an impressive number of starred restaurants, everyone thinks that in Japan you can only eat well in restaurants that fit these Western standards. Nothing is further from the truth.

Atsu atsu gyushabu

For me, Japan is a treasury full of small, almost impossible to find, neighbourhood restaurants where insanely delicious *local food for local people* is served. Very far from neo-jungle cities such as Tokyo, Osaka, Nagoya and Yokohama, although sometimes very close, tucked away in small alleys, in villages or in the country.

One of the first things I try to do whenever I am in South Asia is to go eat a bowl of hearty noodle soup in one of the countless noodle shops. I gives me a sort of homey feeling, a welcome to Asia disguised in a bowl of soup.

As are many Japanese cuisine elements, this dish also seems very simple, but that is precisely where it is difficult. Simplicity is not simple.

The basic ingredients are a bouillon, noodles, and a few fresh vegetables, some fish and/or meat, and herbs. It sounds very simple but the fact that this delicious, steamy noodle soup very rarely has the same great feel and flavour as in Asia, has convinced me that we are absolutely not taking this delicacy seriously.

It is a bit like in the brilliant Japanese film *Tampopo:* I am also continuously in search for the perfect noodle soup. Such a bowl containing only ingredients that make you really happy. Of course, every chef has his own interpretation: a good example is the thick reduction of chicken and dashi bouillon that is served in the teeny ramen restaurant Kagari in Tokyo, with perfect house-made ramen.

Udon was first made on Sanuki island. I could hardly imagine that the traditional makers of udon have refined their product so well that you simply eat it as it is. Perfectly cooked, with a few drops of a good soy sauce, and you have a fabulous dish. It is precisely this simplicity that requires great skills and expertise.

Koya is such a jewel of a noodle shop, although in the centre of Soho. Udon is made here according to Sanuki's recipe: a subtle, nicely layered dashi is very carefully and slowly extracted from only the very best katsuobushi and large konbu leaves.

The combination is heavenly. Beautiful, perfect udon with the typical bite, a little bit of perfectly poached beef, finely chopped leeks and for the connoisseur, an onsen tamago, a poached egg. This onsen tamago, literally 'egg from the spa' is a very old precursor of low temperature cooking. Eggs were placed in warm water springs so they would cook slowly in mineral-rich water.

Here, they call this cooking method atsu atsu. Literally it means 'heat-heat': the cooked udon, still warm, is covered with warm bouillon. In many Japanese dialects, atsu atsu also means to be passionately in love with someone, this literally hot hot. In this case, I can honestly say that I am totally atsu atsu.

Koya means 'small house'. It may be small in size but the focus and dedication that you find here is only found in great houses.

ADDITIONAL EATERIES
WEST

ANTIDOTE · £££
12A Newburgh Street, London W1F 7RR
T +44 20 7287 8488
www.antidotewinebar.com
⊖ Oxford Circus
▸ Roasted Guinea Fowl, Cider Sauce

BARRAFINA TAPAS RESTAURANT · £££
54 Frith Street, London W1D 4SL
T +44 20 7813 8016
www.barrafina.co.uk
⊖ Leicester Square
▸ Braised Ox Tongue with crushed Potatoes

DININGS · ££££
22 Harcourt Street, London W1H 4HH
T +44 20 7723 0666
www.dinings.co.uk
⊖ Edgeware Road
▸ Hand picked Cornish Crab with creamy Jalapeño Sauce

HEREFORD ROAD · £££
3 Hereford Road, Westbourne Grove
London W2 4AB
T +44 20 7727 1144
www.herefordroad.org
⊖ Bayswater
▸ Roast Leg of Lamb Celeriac Anchovy

JEN CAFÉ · ££
4-8 Newport Place, London WC2H 7JP
⊖ Leicester Square
▸ Pot Stickers

JERK CITY · £
189 Wardour Street, London W1F 8ZD
T +44 20 7287 2878
⊖ Oxford Circus
▸ Jerk Chicken

KAI · £££
65 South Audley Street, London W1K 2QU
T +44 20 7493 8988
www.kaimayfair.co.uk
⊖ Hyde Park Corner
▸ Chilean Sea bass with Snow Leaf

THE LEDBURY · ££££
127 Ledbury Road, London W11 2AQ
T +44 20 7792 9090
www.theledbury.com
⊖ Ladbroke Grove
▸ 4 COURSE TASTING MENU

LOCANDA LOCATELLI · ££££
8 Seymour Street, London W1H 7JZ
T +44 20 7935 9088
www.locandalocatelli.com
⊖ Marble Arch
▸ Marinated Anchovy, smoked Potato, radicchio Salad

MOMO · £££
25 Heddon Street, London W1B 4BH
T +44 20 7434 4040
www.momoresto.com
⊖ Oxford Circus
▸ Couscous Momo

PALM PALACE · ££
80 South Road, Southall, Middlesex UB1 1RD
T +44 20 8574 9209
⊖ Southall
▸ Chicken 65

LA PATISSERIE DES RÊVES · £
43 Marylebone High Street, London W1U 5HE
T 44 20 3603 7333
www.lapatisseriedesreves.com
⊖ Regent's Park
▸ Paris Brest

PEYOTE · ££££
13 Cork Street, London W1S 3NS
T +44 20 7409 1300
www.peyoterestaurant.com
⊖ Piccadilly Circus
▸ Cola Amarillo Laminado

RANDALL AND AUBIN · £££
14- 16 Brewer Street, London W1F 0SG
T +44 20 7287 4447
www.randallandaubin.com
⊖ Leicester Square
▸ Crab Cakes

RASA SAYANG · £££
5 Macclesfield Street, London W1D 6AY
T +44 20 7734 1382
www.rasasayangfood.com
⊖ Leicester Square
▸ Crispy Chicken Wings with Gado Gado

ROYAL CHINA CLUB · ££
40-42 Baker Street, London W1U 7AJ
T +44 20 7486 3898
www.rcguk.co.uk
⊖ Marble Arch
▸ Dim Sum

TPT CAFÉ · £
21 Wardour Street, Chinatown, London W1D 6PN
T +44 20 7734 7980
⊖ Leicester Square
▸ Crab sauteed with salted Eggs

UMU · ££££
14-16 Bruton Place, Mayfair, London W1J 6LX
T +44 20 7499 8881
www.umurestaurant.com
⊖ Oxford Circus
▸ Kombu and Shiso cured Wild Salmon

YOUNG CHEN · £
22 Lisle Street, London WC2H 7BY
T +44 20 7287 3045
⊖ Leicester Square
▸ Siu Mai

ALPHABETICAL INDEX

Colofon

www.lannoo.com
Register on our website to regularly receive our newsletter
with new publications as well as exclusive offers.

Texts: Luc Hoornaert
Photography: Kris Vlegels, except the following pictures with courtesy of Amaya, Cay Tre,
Hakkasan, Goodman, Nobu (Mark O'Flaherty), The Ritz London, Sake No Hana, Sushi-
samba & Yauatcha.
Book design: Grietje Uytdenhouwen
Cover design & illustrations: Emma Thyssen

If you have any questions or remarks, do not hesitate to contact our editorial team:
redactiekunstenstijl@lannoo.com.

© Lannoo Publishers, Tielt, 2015
ISBN: 978 94 014 2482 0
Registration of copyright: D/2015/45/72
NUR: 440/504